Bearded Dragon

2nd Edition

Steve Grenard

BICENTENNIAL
1807
WILEY
2007
BICENTENNIAL

Wiley Publishing, Inc.

Copyright © 2008 by Wiley Publishing, Inc., Hoboken, New Jersey. All rights reserved.

Howell Book House
Published by Wiley Publishing, Inc., Hoboken, New Jersey

For general information on our other products and services or to obtain technical support please contact our Customer Care Department within the U.S. at (800) 762-2974, outside the U.S. at (317) 572-3993 or fax (317) 572-4002.

Wiley also publishes its books in a variety of electronic formats. Some content that appears in print may not be available in electronic books. For more information about Wiley products, please visit our web site at www.wiley.com.

Library of Congress Cataloging-in-Publication Data:
Grenard, Steve.
  Bearded dragon / Steve Grenard.—2nd ed.
    p. cm.—(Your happy healthy pet)
  Includes index.
  ISBN-13: 978-0-470-16511-9 (cloth)
  ISBN-10: 0-470-16511-1
  1. Bearded dragons (Reptiles) as pets. I. Title.
  SF459.L5G755 2007
  639.3'955—c22

                                    2007020117

Printed in the United States of America

10 9 8 7 6 5 4 3 2

Book design by Melissa Auciello-Brogan
Cover design by Michael J. Freeland
Book production by Wiley Publishing, Inc. Composition Services
Wiley Bicentennial Logo: Richard J. Pacifico

About the Author

Steve Grenard is an avid herpetologist with more than forty years of experience with amphibians and reptiles; he published a paper on the reproduction of the Marsupial Frog in 1958. In the summer of 2000, he published a controversial and widely debated review in *Natural History Magazine* on the possibility of American rattlesnake venoms evolving new properties. He is the author of several Howell Book House titles, including: *Your Happy Healthy Pet: Frogs and Toads, An Owner's Guide to a Happy Healthy Pet: Lizard* and *Amphibians: Their Care and Keeping*. He is also the author of a number of scholarly medical and herpetological books, including *Medical Herpetology* and *Handbook of Alligators and Crocodiles,* and is the author of *Introduction to Respiratory Care,* a best-selling text review of respiratory therapy. Steve is a board-certified respiratory therapist and polysomnographer and is the clinical coordinator of the Institute of Sleep Medicine at Staten Island University Hospital in Staten Island, New York.

About Howell Book House

Since 1961, Howell Book House has been America's premier publisher of pet books. We're dedicated to companion animals and the people who love them, and our books reflect that commitment. Our stable of authors—training experts, veterinarians, breeders, and other authorities—is second to none. And we've won more Maxwell Awards from the Dog Writers Association of America than any other publisher.

As we head toward the half-century mark, we're more committed than ever to providing new and innovative books, along with the classics our readers have grown to love. From bringing home a new puppy to competing in advanced equestrian events, Howell has the titles that keep animal lovers coming back again and again.

Contents

Shopping List

You'll need to do a bit of stocking up before you bring your lizard home. Below is a basic list of must-have supplies. For more detailed information on the selection of each item below, consult chapter 6. For specific guidance on what food you'll need, review chapter 7.

- ☐ 30- to 55-gallonlong tank with secure screen top
- ☐ Sturdy tank stand or table
- ☐ Substrate (paper towels, newsprint, rabbit pellets or calcium carbonate sand only)
- ☐ Shallow water dishes (1 inch deep)
- ☐ Food dish (1 to 1.5 inches deep)
- ☐ Basking sites (driftwood, rock, smooth lumber)
- ☐ Climbing places (driftwood logs and branches)
- ☐ Shelter boxes
- ☐ Plants (reptile-safe live plants or artificial plants, which are preferred)
- ☐ Hanging thermometer or thermometer/thermostat

- ☐ Heater (over tank, undertank, or both)
- ☐ Full-spectrum light
- ☐ Spray mister bottle
- ☐ Fresh fruits and vegetables
- ☐ Appropriate live food (bring home with lizard)
- ☐ Holding tank for crickets with secure screen cover and cardboard egg crates as substratum
- ☐ Vitamin and calcium supplements (phosphorus free) for crickets (do not use products with high vitamin A levels) There are likely to be a few other items that you're dying to pick up before bringing your bearded dragon home.

Use the following blanks to note any additional items you'll be shopping for.

- ☐ _____
- ☐ _____
- ☐ _____
- ☐ _____
- ☐ _____

Pet Sitter's Guide

We can be reached at (___)_____-_____ Cell phone (___)_____-_____

_____

We will return on _____ (date) at _____ (approximate time)

Other individual to contact in case of emergency _____

_____

Number of lizards we have: _____

_____

Care Instructions

In the following blank lines, let the sitter know what to feed, how much, and when; what tasks need to be performed daily; and what weekly tasks they'll be responsible for.

Morning_____

_____

_____

_____

_____

_____

_____

Evening _____

_____

_____

_____

_____

_____

Other tasks and special instructions _____

_____

_____

_____

_____

Part I

The Wonderful Lizard of Oz

move quickly. Unlike some other lizards, most agamids are unable to move their tails independently of their bodies. After looking at various kinds of agamids, you will soon be able to discern the family resemblance among them.

The bearded dragons were originally assigned to the genus *Amphibolurus*, a name derived from the Greek that means "a tail that can be lashed this way and that." This name refers to a group of agamid lizards with long, thin, whiplike tails. But it soon became evident that beardies were different from the other lizards in this genus. For one thing, they have shorter tails, and they wag them. Plus, there's the beard. And so, in 1982, an Australian zoologist placed these unique lizards in their own genus, which he named *Pogona*, from the Greek *pogon*, which means "beard."

By this time, the question on everyone's mind is: Do these lizards really have beards? The answer is no . . . at least, not hairy ones. No reptiles have hair. Beardies have a highly distensible throat (called the gular pouch), which is covered on the outside by filamentous floppy processes (flappy sprigs of scale tissue that resemble a beard) emanating from their scales. As the pouch is distended, they are able to erect these filaments in such a way that their head looks much bigger than it is. This is a defensive measure that beardies use to scare off predators, and it usually works. The end result to the human eye, however, is what can best be described as a beard.

The Types of Bearded Dragons

There are eight species of bearded dragons in the *Pogona* genus. The name that follows the scientific species is that of the scientist who first identified, described, and named the species, followed by the year of the discovery. As you can see, all but one species were officially described and identified in the 1900s. This shows how little was known about these lizards until recently.

1. Eastern bearded dragon, *Pogona barbata* (Cuvier, 1829)
2. Dwarf bearded dragon, *Pogona minor* (Sternfeld, 1919)
3. Inland or central bearded dragon, *Pogona vitticeps* (Ahl, 1926)
4. Western bearded dragon, *Pogona minima* (Loveridge, 1933)
5. Small-scaled or Drysdale River bearded dragon, *Pogona microlepidota* (Glauert, 1952)
6. Mitchell's northwest bearded dragon, *Pogona mitchelli* (Badham, 1976)
7. Nullabor bearded dragon, *Pogona nullabor* (Badham, 1976)
8. Rankin's or Lawson's bearded dragon, *Pogona henrylawsoni* (Wells and Wellington, 1985)

Many people like lizards because they look like little dinosaurs.

Bearded dragons are found virtually all over Australia except the extreme north, save perhaps for Lawson's bearded dragon. They are also not found in the extreme south. There is also fossil evidence that a species of this group was flourishing on Kangaroo Island some 10,000 to 16,000 years ago, but is now extinct. Although little is certain about the evolutionary relationship of these lizards, *Pogona barbata, Pogona henrylawsoni, Pogona minima,* and the south-western population of *Pogona minor* all have a yellow or orange mouth.

Eastern Bearded Dragon (*Pogona barbata*)

The word *barbata* is Latin for "bearded." This species was the first bearded dragon discovered, and is one of the largest and heaviest of the bearded dragon clan, with early records of animals growing to 1 foot, 8.5 inches in total length, about 1 foot of which is the tail. Lizards nearing 2 feet long have also been recorded. The Eastern bearded dragon is occasionally available in the pet trade in North America from captive-bred colonies.

In the wild, this lizard is found in eastern and southeastern Australia, but not on the Cape York Peninsula, Queensland, or Tasmania. It is semi-arboreal, preferring to perch on low-lying branches, bushes, and rocky outcrops, which are known as "tors" down under in Oz. It can frequently be seen perched on the tops of fence posts as well.

The Eastern bearded dragon is one of the largest and the heaviest of the bearded dragon clan.

It does well in a variety of habitats, ranging from seasonally wet coastal forests to arid, inland scrublands. It feeds on a variety of flowers and tender leaves, and is frequently also observed basking on roads—a risky way to obtain belly heat.

Dwarf Bearded Dragon (*Pogona minor*)

The dwarf bearded dragon is also found in western Australia. However, it is a smaller species than its western bearded dragon cousin, reaching a maximum body length of about 8 to 10 inches. Its range is from the central coast of Western Australia through central Australia and South Australia to the Eyre Peninsula.

Inland or Central Bearded Dragon (*Pogona vitticeps*)

The inland or central bearded dragon is one of the most common species of bearded dragon, both in Australia as well as in the pet trade. This species is the one you would be most likely to find sold by breeders and pet shops, or at swap meets. The majority of this book on the care, keeping, and breeding of bearded dragons refers to this species.

The inland beardie is widely distributed throughout the noncoastal areas of the eastern states through the eastern half of south Australia and north to southeastern Northern Territory. It is found in a wide range of habitats, from dry forests and scrublands to the sandy deserts. It is semi-arboreal and perches on roadside fence posts and hills, fallen timber, or trees. It dines on vegetable matter, preferring soft leaves and flowers when available. It is also a voracious insect predator and will quickly consume large numbers of crickets or other live insect foods placed in its enclosure.

A long, large, and heavy-bodied group of these lizards is being bred in Germany and they have earned themselves the nickname German Giants.

Western Bearded Dragon (*Pogona minima*)

The western bearded dragon is found over a vast swath of southwestern Australia in a variety of habitats, ranging from coastal sand dunes to heavily forested areas. Its range is from southwestern Australia far into the arid interior. It is semi-arboreal, and in the wild it perches and basks on fallen trees and rocks. Between October and February, it produces one or possibly two clutches of eggs, numbering from five to fifteen per clutch. During this time, this species is found basking on roads, and a great many get run over by cars.

Some of these dragons may be available overseas as a result of previous smuggling. Western beardies reach a maximum length of about 20 inches, which makes this species among the largest of the beardies and not truly an example of the scientific name *minima*—although the scientist who first named this species may have had other reasons for dubbing it *minima*.

The inland bearded dragon is the species found most often in the pet trade.

Who Was Henry Lawson and Why the Uproar?

Henry Lawson (1867–1922) is a famous Australian poet. The scientists Richard W. Wells and C. Ross Wellington, in naming this bearded dragon after Lawson, decided it was high time he was recognized with an Australian lizard of his own. No, Lawson didn't have a beard, but he did have a mustache.

These Australian herpetologists also named species after corrupt politicians, a less than fitting honor for a reputable reptile—and they once even tried naming a reptile after Darth Vader!

In the rules of scientific nomenclature, anyone who publishes a description of a species that has never been described before in writing can name it after whatever or whomever they please. Aussie herpetologist Ray Hoser once named a new species after his dog. In fact, newly described species are frequently named after dogs, because dogs often figure prominently in an animal's discovery.

Henry Lawson's bearded dragon was first described to science in 1985 by Wells and Wellington, although many Australian herpetologists were previously aware of its existence. It was many years before the name *henrylawsoni* was for-

Drysdale River Bearded Dragon (*Pogona microlepidota*)

This lizard is also known as the small-scaled bearded dragon (*microlepidota* is Greek for "small-scaled"). This species is not available anywhere in the world outside of Australia. This lizard is found mainly within an area comprising the Drysdale River National Park in the northernmost corner of western Australia, and other areas nearby. It is found in open woodland, where a type of grass known as spinifex grows, as well as other low-lying ground shrubbery.

Mitchell's Bearded Dragon (*Pogona mitchelli*)

Mitchell's bearded dragon is found in northwestern Australia and is generally not available in the pet trade. Some scientists consider it a subspecies of

mally accepted, with rival scientists petitioning the International Commission on Zoological Nomenclature to suppress all new names proposed by Wells and Wellington. The petition was rejected, and the commission ruled that each new name would be reviewed case by case, based on the usual rules of priority. Thus, their proposed name for the species was ruled as official.

Later names proposed for the species (*Pogona brevis* and *Pogona rankini*) were rejected. Confusion reigned for many years after these events, though, and *Pogona henrylawsoni* can still be found on dealer and breeder advertisements listed incorrectly as *Pogona brevis* or *Pogona rankini*.

To add greater confusion to the saga of Henry Lawson's bearded dragon, some Australian herpetologists believe that the specimens in the United States (which they have never examined) may be an as-yet-unnamed ninth species of bearded dragon. In theory, at least, *Pogona henrylawsoni* is known to live only in the black-soil areas of Queensland. Is the similar specimen from bordering northwest Australia a different species, or merely an extension of the range of Lawson's bearded dragon?

Pogona minor. It is a small species, reaching a maximum body length of about 8 inches. Its range is from the lower Northern Territory to northwestern Western Australia, and it is found in dry woodlands and scrubland.

Nullabor Bearded Dragon (*Pogona nullabor*)

This lizard is found in the south central and southwest of Australia, principally on the Nullabor Plain. On the coast, it is found on steep cliffs and near caves. It differs from *Pogona barbata* in that this beardie has white bands across the back and tail, which some breeders find desirable. The Nullabor bearded dragon reaches a maximum body length of about 8 to 10 inches and has the smallest geographic range of any species of bearded dragon.

Chapter 2

The Wild Life of the Bearded Dragon

Oz is truly the land of the lizard, with its torrid, wide-open inland deserts (five of them, in fact), all of which support an amazing abundance of lizard life.

When looking at an animal's behavior, you must consider its natural history: temperature regulation, feeding behaviors and diet, courtship, mating, and reproduction, as well as defense against and escape from predators. Understanding these behaviors in the wild will help you successfully maintain such animals in captivity. And, on occasion, the observations of animals in captivity help unravel mysteries that field biologists could never solve.

Temperature Regulation

Understanding how bearded dragons regulate their body temperature is an essential part of keeping them well-fed, healthy, and in tip-top condition. Beardies obtain heat from their surroundings. These kinds of animals are called ectotherms. By contrast, animals who maintain their own body temperatures within a narrow range by producing heat internally are called endotherms. Birds and mammals, including humans, are endotherms. Although all reptiles are ectotherms, some scientists theorize that prehistoric dinosaurs were not ectotherms, and recent research indicates that some sea turtles maintain core temperatures that are warmer than the water in which they live.

Remarkably, under some circumstances reptiles can maintain a fairly constant body temperature (even though they are dependent on their environment

Beardies move in and out of the sun as one strategy to regulate their body temperature.

for ensuring this). Bearded dragons actually regulate their body temperatures carefully during certain times of the day by their behavior. What's more, beardies maintain body temperatures almost as high as that of a bird or mammal. In other words, given the proper conditions, beardies are anything but cold-blooded. Agamid lizards of all types are prevalent in the world's deserts.

Ectothermy enables them to become metabolically inactive when food supplies are scarce. Beardies, in particular, are low-energy animals. A day's food supply for a rodent can last a beardie several days. Beardies do not expend much energy in search of food. They are equally content eating plant matter or insect prey, and they do not run very far or work very hard in pursuit of either. If they find some tender leaves or flowers to eat, they can hang around such a location for hours, eating what they will when they wish.

Day and Night Temperatures

Unlike many reptiles, beardies are active in the daytime, even the hottest parts of the day, and are comfortable with temperatures well into the 90s. They obtain their body heat from the sun, and are constantly shuttling in and out of the sun to regulate their temperature. At night they get heat from the ground

In parts of Australia, beardies have been found burrowed deep under slabs of rock, waiting out the cooler weather.

inactive state, which means that it would be difficult to rouse, and was clearly hibernating.

In other reptiles, breeders of captive animals artificially create conditions that cause hibernation in both sexes before mating and breeding attempts, but this has not been described as a necessity in bearded dragons and it is difficult to say whether it would be beneficial in breeding captive beardies.

Other scientists and advanced beardie hobbyists say bearded dragons also engage in a behavior known as brumation, which is a period of inactivity and even lethargy that may be dictated by a combination of shortened days (something you can control in captivity), extremes of temperature, and a beardie's natural predilection to become lethargic and inactive whenever conditions are not just right.

Brumation is different than hibernation in that it is marked by periodic awakening and temporary resumption of activity and feeding. Hibernation is usually one lengthy period of inactivity where reptiles go underground to escape the cold in wintry weather. Some breeders believe inducing brumation in beardies helps both males and females get ready to mate. (For more about brumation and your pet beardie, see chapter 8.)

Predator and Prey

Bearded dragons inhabit arid scrubland, where food resources may be scarce, so they can't afford to be picky eaters—and they aren't. Beardies are omnivores, which means that they relish both animal and vegetable matter and can live on either or a combination of both. Because bearded dragons consume large quantities of either vegetable or insect matter, as available, they must have large stomachs to handle the load. Their appetites are accommodated by their tank-like body, but this decreases their ability to run and escape from predators. As a result, natural selection favored a spiny body form and the expandable "beard" as antipredator mechanisms, rather than the sleek, long, torpedolike body of other lizards capable of escaping at great speeds.

Beardies, who are active in the daylight and spend prolonged periods in the open foraging on vegetation or the occasional insect passerby, are clearly at increased risk of being preyed upon. Their beards, their spiny bodies, and their sandy coloration give them some ability to blend in with their surroundings, which helps protect them.

Freeze or Fight

Beardies also show an unusual reluctance to move, even when directly threatened by a predator. This works to their advantage, as movement tips off predators as to their exact location and negates the effectiveness of their camouflage. This laid-back nature is one of their more endearing traits as captive pets. They can be approached, picked up, and kept perched on a human hand or arm for prolonged periods and they hardly flinch. It is not exactly fair, therefore, to characterize beardies as tame or especially calm. It's just their standard behavior; this behavior is the same behavior they would adopt if they were confronted by an enemy, and anything larger than they are (and that includes people) is apt to trigger this reaction.

If, on the other hand, a predator in the wild confronts a beardie at close range, the lizard will respond by blowing out its fake whiskers, flattening its body close to the ground, and opening its mouth in a color-flashing gape. If all this doesn't work and it is actually attacked, a beardie will fight back. Beardies are truly the "gentlemen" (and "ladies") of the lizard world. First they try camouflage and freezing, then bluffing (displaying the beard and gaping), and only fight as a last resort.

The camouflage and freezing techniques are particularly important to the gravid female (one who is carrying eggs). Bearded dragons produce relatively large clutches of eggs, as often as two or three times a year. I knew of one female

Beardies make laid-back pets, and will perch on an arm for quite a while.

inland bearded dragon who produced fifty-six eggs in one year in two separate clutches. Such a high number of eggs, representing perhaps as much as one-third of her total body mass, is undoubtedly a direct consequence of this lizard's robust body form. Sleek, fast-moving lizards, such as anoles and geckos, produce between one and two pea-sized eggs per clutch. But a beardie weighed down by twenty-five or more eggs (each about half the size of a ping-pong ball) cannot be expected to move that quickly. As a consequence, it is obvious that gravid female beardies rely almost entirely upon freezing and camouflage, rather than beard display, to fool enemies; rather than challenge an enemy they cannot escape from, they figure it's better to just play possum.

Beardie Social Interactions

After studying your bearded dragon in its captive home, you may soon become aware that it visually follows your every move. If food or a lizard in an adjoining cage comes into sight, your beardie will become very attentive. Beardies and other agamids use their sight more than any other sense. This is because they are active in the daytime (diurnal). They forage out in the open, and so must be able to spot predators or food at great distances.

Because adult bearded dragons have subtle sexual differences among males and females that are visually discernible, beardies also use their vision to detect potential mates. Social interactions among bearded dragons consist of a unique

Social interactions among beardies consist of a set of visual signals.

set of movements that can only be construed as visual signals. Social behavior involves a number of changes in arm or leg position, body shape, color, and even color patterns. The head is bobbed up and down when mating occurs, and the throat may be distended and the body raised, with the animal elevating itself off the ground. Beardies also compress or depress their sides.

Waving

Waving is one of their most endearing (to humans) visual signals. The beardie will rest on three legs and raise one of its front arms, then slowly wave it about in a circular motion as if they were waving hello or good-bye to a friend! It is not clear whether this is a greeting, a sign of submission, or some sort of secret signal indicating to another lizard that it is a friend, not a foe.

> **Another Beardie Nickname**
>
> The bearded dragon's arm waving is referred to by scientists as circumduction. This behavior has also earned beardies the nickname "ta-ta lizards," after the British colloquial expression that means "so long" or "good-bye."

The uncanny resemblance of this bearded dragon behavior to human arm waving is so remarkable that you would have to see it firsthand to believe it. Although I have witnessed this behavior in isolated beardies, it is even more

Introducing nonnative species into Australia put severe pressure on the native wildlife. In response, Australia banned all imports and exports of animals and plants.

settlers who thought they could be used to traverse Oz's vast deserts), feral cats and dogs, and a plague of nonnative rabbits that eat most types of vegetation in their path.

A type of large toad, known down under as the cane toad (also known as the giant tropical or marine toad, *Bufo marinus*), was introduced to eat sugar cane beetles. Instead, the toad has reproduced unchecked in the millions and eats not only insects but also other Australian wildlife, plus they're very efficient at eating up the food supply of native species. Moreover, native animals (including reptiles) eat the toads and, as they have no immunity to the toad's toxic secretions, they die.

Oz Prohibits Exports

In the 1950s, various Australian states started passing strict laws prohibiting the import and export of any plant or animal life. The prohibition became national law in the early 1960s, and since then it has been illegal to collect, keep, or export any Australian wildlife without a permit. Export permits are extremely difficult to obtain.

Rather than targeting individual endangered or threatened species, the Australian government felt it was simpler to enact a total ban. Although some species are extremely common in Australia (including many species of bearded dragons), they, too, are included in the ban. The law certainly simplified things administratively, but has caused great difficulties for hobbyists and scientists. It also sent the animal trade underground and gave rise to smuggling and official corruption, in which enforcement officers were paid to look the other way or were even involved in illegal animal deals themselves.

Critics of Australia's wildlife laws point out that by forcing all trade to go through smugglers, critically endangered species, as well as common species, escape detection when they are being illegally collected and or exported. In the end, the illegal activity hurts the endangered species rather than pro-

The Tragedy of Smuggling

When animals are smuggled, they are often subjected to inhumane and crowded conditions. They may be trussed up for days or even weeks without food or water, as part of legal shipments of canned goods or dry goods. Birds are tied up and their beaks taped shut so they will keep quiet. Smuggled turtles are taped around their shells and stacked like books in crates barely big enough to contain them.

Another ploy is to smuggle out eggs instead of the animals themselves. Eggs need precise conditions of temperature and humidity to thrive. Such conditions in a smuggling operation are impossible to provide and most perish before ever hatching. But a few get through by random luck so the smuggler can get his "payday."

To fight wildlife smuggling, do not buy such animals, ever.

---

tecting them, while protecting some species that don't really need protection. Moreover, because trading in rare and endangered species is more profitable to the smugglers, it is these species that are the prime targets of illegal exports.

It is rumored that some relief from these strict regulations may be forthcoming in the form of a government plan to establish breeding colonies of selected species that are particularly popular worldwide. These animals could then be exported—to the ultimate benefit of the country and its export trade. If this does happen, bearded dragons are likely to be one of the first species selected.

There is a precedent for such a program in Central America, where there are government-permitted breeding farms for the common green iguana. The iguanas are being bred for food and leather as well as to support the pet trade worldwide.

The pioneer of iguana farming is Dr. Dagmar Werner, who started the Pro Iguana Verde Foundation. She is currently working with six Panamanian communities and others in Costa Rica, Honduras, and Guatemala. Other countries that have expressed interest in her program include El Salvador, Nicaragua, Colombia, and Venezuela. The foundation has established Iguana Park in Orotina, Costa Rica.

If government-supported breeding colonies were established in Australia, beardies could be legally exported—enhancing the genetic health of captive-bred animals worldwide.

The Belize Zoo has also started an iguana breeding program, designed so the typical Belizean can raise iguanas for food. And in the La Mosquitia rain forest in Honduras, there is an Iguana Vigilantes group, whose motto is "The iguana is our heritage, our future. We have to take care of it."

Such captive-breeding operations remove the incentive to collect these animals from the wild, and therefore protect them in their natural habitat. Wild-caught reptiles are less likely to be as healthy or as well-acclimated as captive-bred animals. However, the beardie gene pool is small and getter smaller, since no new wild-caught stock is introduced into the captive-breeding programs established outside Australia. By setting up captive-breeding programs in Australia using new stocks, the gene pool for captive breeding will be much larger and more robust.

If a legitimate breeder charges a few dollars more for a healthy, well-nurtured specimen, as opposed to a wild-caught one, you definitely get your money's worth. The animal will be healthier and less likely to suffer from stress in captivity. It is hoped that one day all trade in wild-caught animals will cease and that trade in exotic animals will be restricted to carefully designed, government sanctioned, and humane breeding programs.

How the Bearded Dragon Left Oz

In view of Australia's restrictive policies on wildlife exports, one question arises: How did bearded dragons end up in North America, Europe, Japan, and elsewhere? Obviously, beardies, along with many other Aussie reptiles, such as the popular frilled dragon and a wide assortment of snakes, were smuggled out.

According to Ray Hoser, the author of two books detailing the illegal export of Australian animals, most bearded dragons were smuggled out of the country between 1974 and 1990. These were either stolen from licensed keepers in the country or seized by government wildlife officials in New South Wales. Hoser says the animals were transported through southeast Asia and then on to Europe, Japan, and North America, where they obtained legal status after being declared to be the product of captive-breeding programs in those countries. These animals formed the foundation stock for the animals in the pet trade outside Australia today.

Authorities have documented a number of routes and methods used by smugglers to get reptiles and birds (and their eggs) out of Australia illegally. But obviously, the large number of these animals that appeared in Europe, the United States, and Japan from the mid-1970s to the early 1990s indicate that a good deal of smuggling took place that escaped detection.

Most bearded dragons available in the pet trade today are descendants of animals smuggled out of Australia between 1974 and 1990.

Smuggling Stories

In his book *Smuggled: The Underground Trade in Australia's Wildlife*, Ray Hoser recounts from a press report the case of John Nichols: "On 17 December 1991, John Francis Nichols, a well known wildlife dealer, was arrested with a friend by Customs Officials at Melbourne Airport, attempting to board a flight to New Zealand with 74 shingleback lizards and seven bearded dragons (*Pogona vitticeps*). The lizards were packed into two suitcases, with their feet taped and hidden under a blanket, when discovered by Customs officials."*

At the time, it was obvious that the lizards would be "laundered" and exported from New Zealand, since New Zealand had not yet tightened up its wildlife regulations. Today, this would be illegal. In another case, according to Hoser's records, Peter and Rosaleen Robson of Freemantle, Australia, posted packages containing western bearded dragons (*Pogona minima*) to reptile dealers in Denmark and Germany. The animals were intercepted before leaving Australia.

(*Reprinted with permission: Hoser, Raymond, *Smuggled: The Underground Trade in Australia's Wildlife*. Sydney, Australia: Kotaki Publishing, 1992.)

Tall Tales

There are some totally absurd stories that allegedly account for the existence of such animals outside of the Australia. One of the most common statements made by criminals is that the animal in question did not come from Australia at all but from nearby Papua New Guinea. This is a half-truth, as Papua New Guinea served as a common transit route for smugglers, as did New Zealand not too long ago. Animals were easily transported by small private boats from northern Australia to Papua New Guinea. From there, they were then exported into the western part of this island, a state called Irian Jaya, which is part of Indonesia.

Many smuggled animals ended up in the hands of hobbyists who are adamantly opposed to smuggling. They just want to see the lizards well cared for.

From Irian Jaya, Indonesian animal exporters and freight consolidators shipped the animals to the Netherlands. Indonesia is a former Dutch colony, so there is a free flow of trade between the two nations. Once in the Netherlands, the animals were legally dispersed all over Europe (a common destination was Germany) and exported to other countries, such as the United States. Since bearded dragons are not native to any country except Australia, beardies in those countries are not covered by the laws of such countries. There is no customs control when moving from one European Union country to another, and breeders received smuggled animals, bred them, and thus produced legal captive-bred offspring to sell outside the EU. Other animals besides beardies are part of this trade as well.

While it is true that some Australian species are also naturally found in Papua New Guinea, there are differences among the animals, and with a little bit of knowledge, they can be easily discerned. This is a moot point now, however, because Papua New Guinea has also shut its borders to the export of reptiles and amphibians.

Another favorite fabrication is that an animal is a long-term captive or the descendant of captive-bred animals that were exported from Australia before all exports were banned. But the ban went into effect more than thirty-five years

Hope for the Future

The Sydney Herald in Australia ran a story on July 6, 1998, announcing that a major Australian Senate inquiry into the com-mercial use of Australian wildlife is likely to recommend that export controls on native animals and plants be relaxed. The inquiry has sparked a debate about the best way to control ani-mal smuggling. It recommends that export bans be lifted for the first time since they became an Australian national policy back in the early 1960s. However, only birds and other animals that are captive-bred by licensed breeders are apt to fall within the proposed law.

Some senators are also calling for a hefty export tax on such exports, proceeds of which would be used to promote wildlife conservation in Australia and to support a system of enforce-ment concerning captive breeding facilities. The added export tax is also likely to spur breeding attempts by overseas buyers, who would gladly pay such fees to inject new genetic vigor into an aging and overworked gene pool among existing overseas stocks that are based on confiscated smuggled animals.

As of 2007, the recommendations were still being debated.

a small schoolchild was arrested for scooping up some tadpoles to observe for science class.

If any native reptiles are to be legally exported from Australia, it makes sense that the number-one draft choice should be bearded dragons. Most species of bearded dragon are neither rare nor endangered. The fact that tens of thousands die on the country's highways has had no impact on their numbers in the wild, and captive-breeding programs of this easy-to-breed lizard, both within the country as well as those already established overseas, would keep wild-caught numbers to a minimum. In any case, the numbers permitted for captivity or export could still be regulated by authorities if the laws were changed.

Australia lags far behind the United States and Europe in the captive care and husbandry of one of its own most populous native lizards. The reasons for this include laws that make it difficult or impossible to legally own bearded dragons (why risk prison for a lizard?) and the abundance of these animals in the wild, making them less desirable or interesting to keepers. According to Hoser, Australian herpetologists have added to their knowledge of captive care of bearded dragons from publications from the United States and Europe, a truly ironic situation.

While all hobbyists agree that the collection of wild-caught specimens should be minimized or eliminated by the proliferation of captive-bred animals, Aussie herpetologists admit that at present and for the foreseeable future, beardies are no longer in danger. Their greatest threats are automobiles, natural predators, and habitat encroachment by humans. Even in the last case, populations of these dragons have managed to survive, side by side with humans, and in no apparent distress.

Beardies are not endangered in Australia and make great pets. These are two good arguments for carefully supervised breeding and export programs in Oz.

Part II
Your Pet
Bearded Dragon

Chapter 4

The Biology of Beardies

Bearded dragons are four-legged, spiny lizards that are more or less shaped like a disk or a tank, with a rounded body that lies close to the ground. They are physically well adapted to arid, desertlike conditions and are found in a variety of dry habitats, ranging from desert to plains and scrublands to forested areas. Their sandy coloration and blotchy patterns give them excellent camouflage. Those that live in red, sandy areas develop a reddish coloration that improves their ability to conceal themselves.

Beardie Anatomy

Skin

The skin of bearded dragons is rough and bumpy or leathery. It contains many soft spines that make these animals somewhat unpalatable to larger predators. Their skin bumps are useful in obtaining water. Beardies live in areas where rain or standing fresh water is scarce to nonexistent. When it does rain, the water washes through the beardie's bumpy, scaly skin and pours down onto its snout. Beardies have been observed standing in the rain, their bodies widely spread and pointed toward the rainfall. They lower their heads below body level and, as the rain runs onto their snout, they lick it off or catch it with their tongues.

Limbs

Bearded dragons have four robust legs with five clawed toes on each foot. The claws are relatively soft, and handlers are rarely, if ever, scratched by them. The

A bearded dragon will shed its skin, or molt, from time to time.

front claws are used to help them climb to the tops of such basking objects as fence poles and tree trunks. The rear toes dig into these objects so the beardie does not fall off.

The female uses her clawed feet to dig a nest in which to lay her eggs. The female scoops out a hole long enough to bury herself in. She deposits her eggs and then emerges, carefully covering the entrance over before she departs.

Tail

All bearded dragons have a moderate-size tail that is wide at the base and tapers toward the tip. Many lizards have a defense mechanism called caudal autotomy, which means dropping the tail. Special muscles make the detached tail wiggle and writhe, keeping the predator from noticing that the best part of the meal is getting away! In most lizards, this occurs within a vertebra along a specially developed fracture plane. Bearded dragons may also lose their tails, but they do not have this fracture plane. Instead, their tail can snap off between vertebrae at their natural separation points.

A beardie can also lose its tail by having it bitten off, either by another bearded dragon or by a predator. If this happens, the remaining tail will heal up.

Nineteenth-century Australian zoologists wrote that beardies would use their tails in a whipping motion to defend themselves. However, this seems not to be the case. Beardies are not known to actively strike human handlers with

Beardies have some teeth that are adapted for eating insects and some teeth that are adapted for eating plant matter.

their tails (at least mine never have). If tail whipping were a common defense, you would expect to see it used when the lizards are handled by humans.

Teeth

Beardies, like all the lizards in the Agamidae family, have all but their front teeth fused to the sides of their jaws, an anatomical feature known as acrodonty. These front teeth fall out and grow back in at regular intervals, but the fused teeth are there for life.

The two kinds of teeth seen in beardies and other agamid lizards accommodate the wide diversity of their diets. The replaceable front teeth are cone-shaped or pointed, and are used for grasping and piercing live prey. The permanent teeth behind them are compressed or chisel-shaped and are better suited to cutting and slicing—just what a lizard needs to eat plant matter.

Beardie Physiology

Circulatory System

Like most reptiles, bearded dragons have a three-chambered heart. Their anatomy enables them to change the pattern of blood flow within the head and body to help them control their temperature. When they first emerge into the daylight in the morning, they divert blood to large sinuses in the head. This heats up the beardie's brain and sensory organs first, for maximum functioning early in the day. When they bask with their back facing the sun, their dorsal blood vessels dilate and their heart rate increases, which also helps speed up the transfer of heat throughout the body.

Digestive System

The digestive system of bearded dragons begins with the oral cavity and teeth. Unlike many herbivorous reptiles, beardies chew their food using their teeth, releasing nutrients and aiding in the digestion of vegetable matter. Food is swallowed and sent to the stomach via a relatively short esophagus.

In the stomach and the intestines, the food is more thoroughly digested and is subjected to fermentation, a specialized type of digestion used by animals that consume significant amounts of vegetable matter. Fermentation requires the presence of bacteria in the gut. Unlike herbivorous mammals (for example, horses, cows, and rabbits), reptiles do not suckle their young following birth. Accordingly, newborn bearded dragons must obtain the bacteria necessary to help ferment and digest their food by ingesting bits of soil that contain feces. In captivity, therefore, newborn beardies should be started on a diet of small insects (pinhead crickets or fruit flies) until they have built up sufficient numbers of this kind of bacteria to obtain nutritional benefit from a vegetarian diet. It can be obtained from their own fecal material, which serves as a culture medium and then is reingested. The insects they eat carry this bacteria as well.

The intestinal tract terminates in an all-purpose cavity called the cloaca. It terminates at an anal portal through which waste products are discharged. The cloaca is also used for sexual intercourse, and the female's eggs pass through it as she lays them.

Reproductive System

The reproductive system of beardies is similar to that of all other lizards. It consists of paired internal gonads (ovaries in females, testes in males). The female's ovaries are connected to the cloaca by oviducts; the male's testes by a specialized intromittent organ known as a hemipenes, which is located inside the cloaca but which can be averted outward to accomplish true internal fertilization of the female's eggs during mating.

Urinary System

Urinary wastes are processed by a pair of kidneys and empty into the cloaca for excretion by the ureters. As discussed earlier, beardies often go for long periods of time without water and may obtain what little water they can from their food.

> **TIP**
>
> As a desert species, beardies survive well in the absence of rainfall or drinking water, but captives should be sprayed lightly several times a week. Beardies also obtain water from their food, and their vegetable meals can be easily sprayed down with water.

Thus, they must be able to conserve fluids. To rid themselves of waste products while retaining fluids, beardies and other reptiles with a similar problem excrete dry urine, which appears as a chalky, white, powdery substance consisting largely of the nitrogenous waste product called uric acid.

When the liquid urine enters the bladder or the cloaca, water is reabsorbed into the body. This process in reptiles enables them to excrete nitrogenous waste products with little or no fluid lost in the process. This material, along with fecal wastes, is emptied to the outside via the cloaca.

Beardie Senses

Experiments performed on captive beardies indicate that they have excellent hearing, and they stand alert when they hear loud or unusual noises. When they hold their bodies close to the ground, they can also detect ground vibrations, a sense that gives them warning of large predators in the vicinity. This ability does not seem to extend to pavement—when absorbing heat from roadways, a significant percentage of beardies get run over.

We don't know much about the beardie's sense of touch, but we do know they have a sense organ that humans lack: the vomeronasal organ (also known as

When beardies hold their bodies close to the ground, they can detect ground vibrations.

The Beardie's Biological Clock

Bearded dragons have a small, light-sensitive "third eye," also known as the pineal eye. The pineal eye is located between their eyes and beneath the parietal scale on the top of their head. This organ detects solar radiation. Sensory input thus received triggers the release or inhibition of hormones, such as melatonin and prolactin, which control the animal's daily cycle of activity, or circadian rhythm. This organ is, in effect, the lizard's biological clock.

Not all reptiles have this organ. It is absent in crocodilians, several families of lizards, snakes, and turtles. No bird or mammal has such an organ, either, at least not one that functions in exactly this way, although they do have a pineal gland.

the Jacobson's organ), located in the roof of the mouth. This organ, also found in snakes as well as in other lizards, some frogs and toads, and some mammals, functions like a cross between the sensory organs of taste and smell. The vomeronasal organ consists of two fluid-filled sacs that connect to the nasal cavity via the nasopalatine ducts, and it processes scents in a different way than the nasal passages.

Unlike snakes and monitor lizards, however, beardies rarely use tongue flicking to check out the palatability or suitability of a plant or a bug as a food item. They seem to rely almost entirely on their vision for this. (Because snakes have very poor vision, they depend on the chemical clues they pick up by tongue flicking—clues that are interpreted by the vomeronasal organ.)

Beardies' eyes are mounted on the sides of their head, leaving them with little or no binocular vision. Yet they can detect food, enemies, or mates at distances of 100 feet. There are apparently no detailed studies concerning their ability to see colors. I have observed, however, that they seem to discern certain colors and select food items based on their color. In particular, they appear to see reds and yellows well—the colors of flowers that are a favorite food.

Chapter 5

Choosing a Pet Bearded Dragon

According to Agama International (a very large-scale lizard-breeding facility), bearded dragons and other related lizards in the Agamidae family are rapidly gaining in popularity and may surpass iguanas in the not too distant future as the most common lizard pets. Agama International estimates that about 100,000 baby bearded dragons are hatched and sold in North America annually. Breeders almost always sell out entire clutches within a few weeks of being hatched, so if you want to obtain your dragons this way, you may have to put yourself on a waiting list!

Before buying your bearded dragon, make sure you are ready. That means doing all your shopping in advance. Before you bring your beardie home, you'll need to take care of some chores.

- Housing setup ready and waiting, including lighting, heating, and all tank furnishings.
- A small supply of food on hand, including live foods, and a reliable, steady source established in advance.

Bring Home a Healthy Beardie

Although adult bearded dragons (6 to 12 inches in length) and adolescents (4 to 8 inches in length) are occasionally for sale, most of the time you will be offered baby beardies measuring about 3 to 4 inches, including the tail. When selecting your pet, make sure that the animal is at least 4 to 6 weeks old (if possible) and

eats both insect and plant matter
with relish. If possible, ask the seller
to feed the beardie in front of you.

Baby beardies should be fat,
active when "spooked" or prodded,
and have a full tail. Both eyes should

be wide open. There should be no obvious eye, mouth, or jaw problems (see chapter 8 for signs of these problems), and no skin bumps other than the normal tubercles and bumpy processes found on these lizards.

Because beardie babies are apt to nibble on one another, make sure your acquisition has all five toes, complete with tiny claws, on all four feet. Be especially wary of sellers (pet shops, swap-meet vendors, or private breeders) who keep a bunch of baby dragons together in the same tank, as this practice tends to result in injured stock.

Some bearded dragons will dominate others, prevent them from eating, and will attack those who get in their way. In fact, it is an excellent idea to buy such a dominant lizard, if you can identify it. Just make sure you house it by itself.

Turn the baby beardie over and inspect its anal region. Make sure there are no feces or similar matter sticking to this area and that it is clean. Also check for the presence of feces in the enclosure. It should be solid or semisolid and

You're most likely to end up with a baby. Make sure your pet is healthy and a hearty eater.

bearded dragon. Selective breeding efforts have also resulted in baby beardies with reddish or golden heads and standard bodies.

Interestingly, some color variations, even if genetically based, are also dependent on dietary factors. An example of this occurred many years ago at the New York Zoological Society in the Bronx, which had a colony of pink flamingos that were turning white. Zoo scientists soon discovered that these birds would retain their pink coloration if fed a diet rich in beta-carotene, a vitamin that was found in abundance in their diets in the wild but that was missing from their bird chow-based diet. Reddish, yellowish, orange, or golden beardies may also depend on beta-carotene to maintain their coloration over time. Because beta-carotene and its close associate, vitamin A, can be toxic in high doses, they should be provided only once every two weeks in a scaled-down dose acceptable to a reptile of the beardie's size and type.

> **TIP**
> Bearded dragons with unusual colors sell for more money.

Breeders who imported fresh stock from Germany some years ago also noticed that some of the inland bearded dragons they received were unusually large and heavy bodied, with lengths exceeding 2 feet. Dubbed German giants, these varieties were much bigger than standard beardies and had an iris that was silvery-gold. These gigantic bearded dragons also tend to produce unusually large clutches of up to sixty eggs at a time.

Designer Beardies

For many years, snake breeders have been experimenting with cross-breeding various natural color variations to obtain unusually patterned and colored snakes that do not, nor could, exist in the wild. These unusual reptiles are dubbed "designer snakes." Breeders are beginning to do the same with bearded dragons.

This beardie's atypical coloring is a product of selective breeding to create color variations that do not occur in the wild.

One prominent, longtime breeder of beardies is developing these "designer beardies":

- Vivid orange eyelids with yellow facial highlights
- Orange beards with light buff brown bodies
- Juveniles with orange spots running down the back
- Barred side patterns leading to orange tiger-stripe beardies

It won't be long before we'll have the same sort of beardie varieties that have been developed in snakes: Creamsicle beardies, zigzag beardies, black beardies, blue beardies, albino beardies, and other variations we cannot even imagine. Whether this creative breeding will be good for the captive bearded dragon gene pool, a very limited resource remains to be seen.

Some are breeding the unusually hardy German giants mentioned above with some of the more colorful bearded dragons in the hope of creating color variations that are beautiful as well as strong.

The superior resistance to infectious disease of the German giants is particularly noteworthy, and is believed to be the result of many years of careful captive breeding and the development of increasingly strong immune responses. If this work proves nothing else, it is that animals held in captivity are exposed to different sorts of infectious threats than those in the wild. This was demonstrated when these German giants were bred with the progeny of recently captured wild-caught beardies. The early generations, at least, were not particularly more hardy or disease-resistant than one would expect. Based on these experiments, conferred immunities are apt to take many generations of captive breeding efforts to be fully realized.

> **Dragons Go Hollywood**
>
> The attraction of beardies has reached to the stars. According to *PetLife* magazine, Leonardo DiCaprio keeps a bearded dragon named Blizz.

Where to Get Your Bearded Dragon

Local breeders and collectors, mail-order breeders and wholesalers, and local pet shops will all have bearded dragons for sale. Another way of acquiring bearded dragons is to attend swap meets and herp marts, which are held regularly all over the United States and in other countries. There are always a few bearded dragon sellers there among the other reptile dealers.

Breeders

One of the best places to get a bearded dragon is from a local breeder or collector—a person who breeds a small number of animals as a hobby. The advantages are numerous: Most hobby breeders are very conscientious about their animals and take great care in keeping and caring for them. Since the breeder has a wealth of experience in keeping and raising lizards, they will be able to answer any questions you have and pass on useful information and care tips. Price-wise, most hobby breeders are competitive with mail-order dealers, without the shipping costs.

There are a few disadvantages as well, and they must be carefully considered. The biggest problem in dealing with a hobby breeder is finding one. Even if you live in a large city, it is unlikely many reptile breeders will live near you. And, since few local breeders advertise, the only way to find them is through word of mouth. Your local herpetological society should be able to direct you to reputable breeders in your area—if there are any.

Mail Order

If you cannot find bearded dragons for your collection locally, you can buy them by mail order. You can track down breeders and importers of beardies by

Breeders have a lot of experience raising and caring for beardies, and can give you expert advice.

reading the popular magazines about reptiles and amphibians and contacting their advertisers. Breeders can also be found through local herpetological societies.

Beardies are fairly hardy creatures, and shipping them is not difficult. Most dealers will place your bearded dragon inside a cloth bag along with some moss as padding to prevent the lizard from being bounced around. This container is then placed inside a shipping box, with several inches of newspaper or foam peanuts as insulation and padding, and the shipping box is completely sealed with tape to prevent rapid temperature changes. The box will then be marked "Live Lizards."

There is enough air inside the box for a week or so, although most live reptiles reach their destinations overnight.

You should specifically request that the shipping company require a signature from you upon delivery. This prevents the delivery person from simply leaving the box by your front door, where it may be exposed to direct sunlight and become too hot for your lizard, or chilly weather that is too cold.

When your pet arrives, it will be a bit disoriented by the trip, so you should remove it gently from the packaging, place it in the artificial habitat you set up, make sure there is food and water, and then leave it alone for a few days so it can adjust to its new surroundings.

Beardies on the Net

Commercial dealers can be found on the Internet by doing a search for the keywords "bearded dragon breeder" or "bearded dragon prices." (You'll also find some listed in the appendix.) There are even forums devoted solely to beardies. Through these forums you can contact breeders of bearded dragons as well as obtain references on their reliability from third-party members via private e-mail. In the public forum, you can also discuss bearded dragon issues, ask about care and keeping, and perhaps even find takers for the results of your own breeding projects. Why not share your own experiences—both good and bad—with fellow bearded dragon enthusiasts? This is a fun and educational way to learn more about bearded dragons as well as to offer advice based on your own efforts.

A breeder may ask you to send a deposit on your purchase from a future clutch. For your own protection, be sure to ascertain their policies and terms before you buy, to prevent any misunderstandings. If you want to see the animal before you buy it, then your next best option is to attend a large local or national swap meet or wait until your local pet store obtains some bearded dragons.

Beardies love to climb, so they will need a high enclosure. These are young lizards, but as they get older, they may not be so amenable to community housing.

becomes excessive but permit unfiltered sunlight to rain down on the beardies during the warmer months.

Cage Height—How High Is High?

Height is important because beardies love to climb and perch on posts and branches. In a captive situation, the enclosure should be at least 2 to 2.5 feet high. Remember that beardies love to do three things: sprint, climb, and perch. Although they will stay in one place for what seems to be hours on end, basking or soaking up the heat from above or from the substrate, there will be times when they would like to take off for a little run or climb among some branches that are heavy enough to support them.

Community Caging?

Bearded dragons are territorial. If you are keeping more than one lizard in the same enclosure, you must give them plenty of room to call their own, including separate feeding stations. You may, nonetheless, find that you have to separate them as you notice the submissive beardies becoming weaker or injured by attacks made by the dominant member(s) of the group.

Cage Cover

Besides keeping beardies and feeder insects such as crickets in, covers keep inquisitive children and household pets out. They are also useful for placing basking lights and full-spectrum lighting (see below). Outdoors, covers are a must to protect your lizards from cats, dogs, opossums, raccoons, birds, and other predators.

A mesh screen is the cover of choice for your beardies—screening allows for plenty of needed ventilation and permits unfiltered sunlight or artificial ultraviolet (UV) A and B light to shine through. Never use a glass cover, which blocks UV rays. Moreover, glass covers cause the air to stagnate and humidity and noxious gases to build up, which could be harmful to your beardies. Because they retain heat and humidity, glass covers also promote fungal growth. And a glass cover can result in overheating the entire enclosure. (In short, a glass top and direct sunlight can cook your lizards!)

Clearly, covers should be made of screening, or "hardware cloth" as it is occasionally called. You can buy one for most aquarium tank sizes in an aquarium supply store. If your cage is an odd size, it may be necessary to build your own frame and cover it with screening yourself.

If your tank is high enough, with at least 6 to 8 inches between the highest perch and the top, you might also consider using no cover at all. While beardies are superb at climbing rough wooden and rocky surfaces, they do not jump, nor can they climb up smooth glass, plastic, or smooth wooden sides of an enclosure, so there is little risk of escape. However, other household pets can get into the cage, and they may not be above trying to eat your beardie or, at the very least, checking it out by biting it.

> **T I P**
>
> If your cover is made of screening, make sure your beardie cannot reach the screen and rub its snout raw trying to nose its way out.

If you have no other pets, you should consider an open top. If there's a perch or a rocky outcrop in the cage, it can be placed in the center, well away from the walls. This way, it cannot serve as a ladder for your beardie to climb over the top.

Substrate

Bottom cover for indoor cages can be as simple as white, unprinted paper towels or unprinted newspaper or a layer of rabbit pellets or Calci-Sand, which is safe if accidentally swallowed. Sterile potting soil is also safe. Astroturf and similar carpet materials have also been advocated as a substrate. If you choose such a substrate,

Calci-Sand comes in a variety of colors and is a safe substrate for your beardie.

the weave must be tight to prevent beardies from catching their nails in the cloth and ripping them off in an attempt to break free.

Many substrates are dangerous to beardies because they may accidentally swallow some of it when eating; because they are indigestible, this can result in intestinal blockage or fecal impaction. Avoid any synthetic particulates, small pebbles, gravel, walnut shells, wood chips, and cedar shavings. One commercial substrate, Calci-Sand, is completely digestible, provides much-needed calcium, and reduces the risk of intestinal blockage.

Plants

Silk or plastic plants are recommended, because your beardies are apt to eat live plants. Although live plants may be more aesthetically pleasing, some may also be toxic to your animals. If you choose to include live plants, make sure they are not toxic. Also be sure to thoroughly wash them before putting them in the cage, because they may have been sprayed with toxic substances.

Artificial plants pose little risk to your beardies and can be quite attractive. They do, however, have to be removed and washed as needed. For ease of handling, all plants should be anchored in their own pots so that they can easily be removed when necessary. Otherwise, you may have to uproot or upset a large amount of your beardie's terrain just to clean the plants.

Beardies Like Beds

Shelter boxes (beds to bearded dragons) are available in both natural rocky designs or as no-frills plastic containers with doorways, that, when turned upside-down, form a shelter for your beardie to sleep in. While these no-frills containers are not pretty, bearded dragons don't seem to care. They serve their purpose well. More elaborate shelters benefit you more than your beardies. They can make do with just about any old shelter, as long as it is big enough to accommodate them and easy to clean.

Cage Furnishings

Beardies love to climb and perch. They like to survey all that they can see from above. Scientists classify them as semi-arboreal because they do not climb high into trees the way truly arboreal animals do, but prefer perches that are just a few feet off the ground.

In a cage, a well-anchored, heavy-duty driftwood branch needs to be only 4 to 6 inches above the substrate for your beardie's climbing enjoyment. You can also construct naturalistic rock formations for your lizard. Beardies will even settle for sitting atop their shelter boxes or leaning against them, backs to the light, to soak up the sun's rays. A variety of naturalistic artificial rock forma-

Your beardie doesn't need to climb very high; it just wants to perch above it all.

Humidity? Don't Sweat It

It is not necessary to acquire humidity-measuring equipment, and you should do nothing to promote humidity buildup. Only the eastern bearded dragon is known to live in habitats with higher than usual relative humidity, but this species and all the rest do best in an arid habitat. Good ventilation of the cage, coupled with minimal water inside, will keep things sufficiently arid for your beardie.

Providing Heat

Wild bearded dragons thermoregulate, thereby sustaining a comfortable body temperature. There is little difference between what happens in the wild and what your beardie does in captivity, save for one big thing—in captivity, you are in charge of the temperature. You control your beardie's thermal environment, cool or hot, so it is important to provide the absolutely best conditions possible. These conditions enable your pet to continue doing what it normally would do if it were scampering around the Australian outback.

To fully understand how heat or cold is provided to captive reptiles, it is helpful to understand how temperature changes or gradients can be provided.

Heat can come from above by:

- Incandescent lights
- Infrared bulbs (heat lamps)
- Nonlight-emitting fixtures, such as screw-in ceramic heaters
- Natural sunlight

Heat can come from below by:

- Electric heating pads
- Heat tape, available in various widths
- "Pig blankets," which are large rubberized or fiberglass-coated heavy-duty heating pads (especially useful for outdoor enclosures)
- Hot rocks

- Standard household heating, such as baseboard heaters, room heaters, and radiators

All electrically powered heating products that produce heat from below can be thermostatically controlled—they will automatically turn on or off, depending on the temperature registered electronically at the surface of the enclosure.

Hot Rocks

Hot rocks, which are ceramic, "naturalistic" stone formations with built-in heating elements, have a reputation of developing hot spots, overheating and burning your reptile. If they are functioning properly and if they do not overheat, hot rocks can be an asset to any lizard that obtains its belly warmth from below.

But be very careful if you give your pet access to hot rocks—your lizard may not consciously be aware that there is too much heat coming from below until that heat permeates its body and reaches higher thermoregulatory centers in the brain. It is this quirk of reptile physiology that has caused reptiles to endure burns on their belly scales before they realize the heating device beneath them is too hot. Because you will not be able to watch your beardie all the time, you are probably better off relying on alternative heating methods.

You'll need a special light socket with a reflector if you decide to provide a heat source from above.

People Thermoregulate, Too

By turning on air conditioners, radiators, electric heaters, standing close to the fire or away from it, taking a cold shower (or a hot one), going into and out of the water (pool, lake, or sea), or escaping the heat with an umbrella or awning, people thermoregulate, too. There is little difference between these human behaviors and the way reptiles thermoregulate. When establishing your lizard's thermal environment, try to remember how you feel when waiting for the bus on a winter day or when you have a power failure in August. Your beardie will appreciate your sensitivity.

Heat from Above

If you opt to use a nonlight-emitting heat source from above, such as an infrared bulb, which emits only red light, or any number of ceramic nonlight-emitting heating coils, you must use specially insulated, heavy-duty reflectors and sockets to absorb the excessive heat produced and to help to prevent fires. No flammable portion of your enclosure should come in direct or even close contact with any of these devices. This includes the plastic frames of all-glass aquariums, the plastic frames of screen covers, the screen covers themselves (especially if they're made of plastic netting), anything made of wood, or anything else that can either melt or burn.

In addition, all cage fixtures should be secure and incapable of toppling over. One unfortunate iguana owner came home to find his house on fire, only to learn later that the fire was started by his lizard! The iguana had knocked over the heat lamp, which was in close proximity to some window curtains. Always think in terms of fire prevention when setting up such arrangements.

Temperature Gradients

All reptile and amphibian enclosures, including those for bearded dragons, must have areas that are hot, areas that are cooler, and areas that are cooler still. These are known as temperature gradients, and bearded dragons must be allowed a choice of locations to rest and remain, each with a different temperature. The

Wild beardies move in and out of the sun to thermoregulate. You will have to provide your pet with warmer areas and cooler areas.

zones of varying temperatures can exist either in the horizontal or vertical plane, although it is much more difficult to arrange them vertically than horizontally. Nature, however, does this quite nicely.

You can achieve a vertical temperature zone in captivity by placing a reflector at one end of the enclosure and an incandescent bulb at the other end, and focusing the light at mid-level straight across the cage. Ground-dwelling reptiles, such as snakes and many terrestrial lizards, do not benefit from layers of heat at different heights. Beardies, as semi-arboreal species, are likely to appreciate having a range of vertical heat levels.

Optimal Beardie Temperatures

Daytime temperatures should range from 80°F to 85°F. Basking spots should be hotter, ranging from 90°F to a maximum of 93°F. At night, the heat source for the basking spots should be turned off. Environmental temperature should be allowed to drop to anywhere from 75°F to 65°F.

If you are the forgetful type or won't be home when the heat from above is no longer needed (usually after nightfall), it may be useful to have fixtures plugged into timers that will turn them off in your absence. Bearded dragons expect temperature drops after nightfall; this is when they become inactive and rest.

Supplemental Heating

If you keep your house cooler at night, especially during the winter in North America, it may be necessary to provide supplemental heating for your bearded dragons. You can do this using red or dark blue incandescent bulbs, infrared bulbs, nonlight-emitting ceramic heating elements, or undercage heating pads or heat tape.

If you know your household temperature is apt to drop below 70°F at night, you can arrange to have these devices turn on by either a timer or a thermostat. Thermostats will shut off the heat element if it overheats while you (and your beardies) are asleep, so this is the preferred alternative. Set the thermostat to cut off the heating elements when temperatures reach 65°F or 70°F. It will turn them back on if temperatures drop below 65°F.

Monitoring the Heat

A good mercury, chemical, or electronic thermometer is a must to accurately monitor the temperature in your bearded dragon enclosure. Trying to estimate the temperature inside an enclosure is impossible, because our body temperature prevents us from evaluating how the temperature feels to the beardie. The best thermometers to invest in are battery-operated, electronic devices with probes that can be inserted into the tank while the read-out remains outside. Check the appendix for dealers who sell this equipment.

Cage Cleaning and Maintenance

Bearded dragons will eat copious amounts of food every day, and they will foul their substrate and water dish (if one is provided) just as rapidly. Therefore, all fecal material and uneaten or leftover vegetable matter should be removed every day. In addition, fouled water bowls should be removed, drained, and rinsed with hot water as needed—probably more than once a day. You should also monitor your heating system and check temperatures throughout the enclosure as part of your daily or every-other-day chores.

At some point, the substrate material will become totally inundated with dried-up bits of uneaten food and small amounts of fecal material and urine that you can't clean up. You will then have to replace it. Cage furniture, such as

It's okay to sometimes let your beardie out of its enclosure, but be sure to first remove any potential hazards from the room and supervise the free time.

shelters, driftwood perches, and rock formations, should also be removed once a week and cleaned. The glass walls of any beardie cage should be wiped down inside and out with paper towels dampened with hot water whenever necessary. Never use any cleansers, soap, window cleaner, or any chemicals. Use plain hot water only. Detergents and chemical cleansers are toxic and could kill your bearded dragon.

Other maintenance chores include watering live plants, trimming off dead leaves, and, if your beardies nibble on them, replacing the entire plant.

Outdoor Housing

In some drier parts of the United States, it may be possible to house your beardies in outdoor enclosures or pens during the warmer months. Such enclosures should provide shelter, be protected from predators such as birds, raccoons, foxes, dogs, and the like, and should be heated at night if temperatures drop below 65°F. A screen cover is the best type of security measure, as long as it fits tightly. It allows your beardies to bask in unfiltered sunlight during the day, and nothing can be healthier for them.

Free Roaming Beardies

A number of lizard owners, such as those with iguanas and large monitor lizards, advocate allowing them to roam free in the house. This is a reasonable idea, but only one secure room should be devoted to roaming lizards, whether adult beardies, iguanas, or monitors. Needless to say, there should be no holes or escape routes large enough for your lizard to slip through.

And while there is no proof beardies shed salmonella, as do other lizards, bear in mind they may do so. Therefore, other pets, such as dogs and cats, as well as small children, toddlers, and babies, should be prohibited from entering such a habitat or playing in it. A lock on the door is a very wise idea if children, dogs, or cats roam free elsewhere in the house.

Many breeders believe an outdoor enclosure helps stimulate breeding cycles, and young beardies will benefit with enhanced growth in larger outdoor enclosures, as well.

Outdoor habitats in areas of heavy rainfall and high humidity might be suitable if you provide the beardies with a high, dry place to shelter from the rain. Indoor greenhouses may have too much humidity unless they are well ventilated, usually by rooftop windows that can be opened.

If you really want to provide a comfortable (and attractive) habitat for your bearded dragons, consider building them a specially designed outdoor vivarium or greenhouse. The enclosure can be planted, landscaped, and have free-flowing water or misting/grass sprinklers (to be used once or twice a day to water plants and provide "rainfall" for beardies to drink). It can be heated by fan-operated gas heaters, electrical heating pads, or even hot water pipes. The frame can be made of treated wood or aluminum, to which a sturdy hardware cloth (preferably rubberized) should be added. The mesh should be small enough to prevent beardies from obtaining a toe-hold and climbing on it, as they might be apt to tear it (creating an escape route) or tear off toenails while moving about.

All outdoor vivariums should be deeply set into the ground, to at least a depth of 18 inches or more, to prevent beardies from tunneling their way out. As a precautionary measure, you may want to place a treated wooden platform

If you live in a warm, dry climate, you may be able to keep your beardie in an outdoor enclosure at least part of the year.

as the outdoor vivarium or greenhouse floor, and cover it with 1 or 2 feet of soil. If the beardies dig in that deep, they will be stopped by the hidden flooring below.

Heat for Outdoor Enclosures

Heating beardie enclosures outdoors in colder climates is not easy. If your heating system fails in the middle of the night when temperatures are plunging into the 20s, 30s, or even 40s, you can wake up to find your beardies dead. It is not recommended that you keep beardies outdoors year-round in any climate where day or nighttime temperatures fall below 65°F.

In some parts of the United States, beardies can be kept in well-protected outdoor compounds virtually year-round, but should be brought indoors on those few days when temperatures may drop below the 60s.

During the day, outdoor enclosures and greenhouses are heated by natural sunlight (if there is sun—if not, artificial, thermostatically controlled heating must be available). Sunlight can overheat a greenhouse during warmer months (in North America, that's March through October), so such structures must

Housing your lizards outside does not mean the end of your cleaning chores. Uneaten food and waste materials should be removed daily.

have roof windows that can be opened or other panels that are screened off but that will permit adequate ventilation or a cooling airflow.

If you live in a climate where keeping lizards outside is not appropriate, you may nonetheless succeed in doing so if you have a heated greenhouse with an alarm that is triggered if the heating system fails. You must be certain that the enclosure will retain heat, even on cold days. Year-round enclosures should be closed on four sides, have a natural or sandy substrate under which heating pads can be placed, and have a screen cover. Caves or upside-down wooden or plastic boxes with entrances cut into them can serve as shelter from the elements. During the winter, the substrate can be enhanced by placing a 1-foot-deep loosely packed layer of alfalfa, which will give beardies the opportunity of digging into the substrate for insulation. If there are heavy rains or snowfall, you must move your beardies indoors for the duration of such harsh weather conditions.

Leaving Beardies Home Alone

Although it is not a good idea to leave any animal home alone for any length of time, you can safely take short trips away as long as your beardies are fed and checked on at least every two days by a substitute caretaker. Unlike some species of fish or amphibians that must be fed daily or even more frequently, beardies can go for two days without food or fresh water (although they'd rather not).

Bearded dragons have developed such resilience to cope with the harsh circumstances of their natural desert or rocky scrubland existence in the wild. Nonetheless, they will eat and drink every day, even several times a day, if given the opportunity. If there is no compelling reason to skip a few days, don't.

Substrate in Outdoor Colonies

Natural grassy or soil substrates should be cleaned regularly. Keep an eye on the substrate to be sure it remains fresh. All uneaten vegetable matter food and fecal material should be scooped up and used in mulch, fertilizer for flower beds, or otherwise properly discarded.

You should routinely rake and turn the soil to a depth of at least 8 inches. By keeping the soil loose, the beardies will be able to dig in if they choose. It is important that they be able to protect and insulate themselves by digging into the substrate—if it becomes hardened and packed down, they may die in the night from cold temperatures. A heated shelter or an underground heating pad will also help prevent such disasters. Temperatures and heating systems including thermostats should be checked at least once a day, preferably just before nightfall.

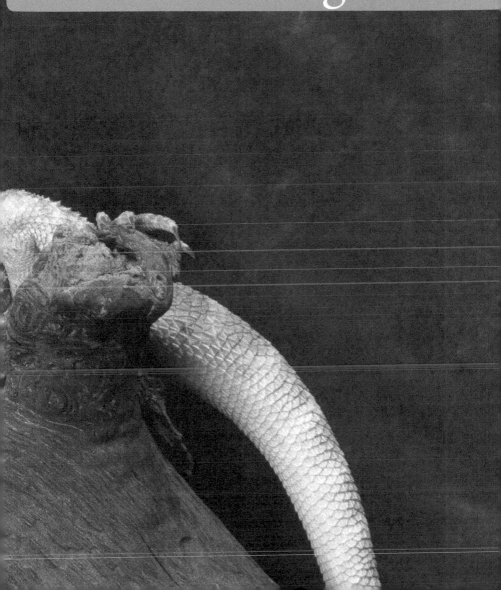

Part III

Caring for Your Bearded Dragon

Chapter 7

Feeding Your Bearded Dragon

Ideally, bearded dragons should be fed and given fresh water every day. Some hobbyists feed their beardies two or even three meals a day. Three meals a day is a healthy feeding schedule for these lizards, if two of those meals consist of greens. It is helpful when discussing beardie feeding and nutrition to understand some special terms that apply to their dietary preferences:

- Omnivorous: eating both animal and vegetable matter
- Foliovorous: leaf eating
- Frugivorous: fruit eating
- Insectivorous: insect eating

Beardies are all of the above and more. Their willingness to consume all types of food is one of the attributes that makes them so easy to care for. They are dietary generalists rather than specialists, and can even be coached to eat specially prepared food out of a jar. Adult bearded dragons will eat baby (and very young) mice. They're also not above eating other lizards, including babies of their own species, so they can also be considered cannibalistic.

Like humans, beardies will eat just about anything they find palatable. But this doesn't mean a steady diet of one food or another is necessarily good for them. Just like people, bearded dragons do best on a varied diet. Fatty, animal-based foods should be fed in moderation. Fortunately, beardies like their vegetables, and fruits and vegetables should form the basis of their diet, with animal-based foods offered two or three times a week to meet their need for animal proteins and other nutritional factors. A well-balanced diet will help your bearded dragon live long and prosper.

Fruits and Veggies

Bearded dragons will eat just about any plant matter, including leaves and fruits as well as bits of whole raw vegetable matter such as carrots. You can observe the unique way bearded dragons chew their food by offering them a baby carrot or a small piece of a larger carrot and watch them chew and pulverize it for swallowing and digestion. Beardies also eat flowers, such as yellow dandelions, and seem attracted to bright colors when eating.

Fruits and vegetables should be chopped into a suitable size, depending on the size of the animal being fed. Baby beardies need finely chopped veggies, juveniles need more coarsely chopped food, and adults can swallow most vegetables in human-size portions with little difficulty.

Among the vegetables recommended for bearded dragons are:

- Carrots (raw and shredded, about 1 to 2 ounces a week)
- Collard greens
- Dandelions (leaves and flowers)
- Frozen mixed veggies (carrots, beans, and peas), thawed
- Hibiscus blooms and other nontoxic flowers (as an occasional treat)
- Kale
- Mustard greens

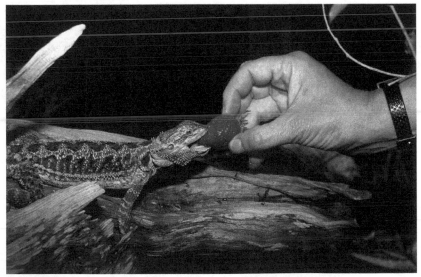

Beardies seem to be attracted to brightly colored foods.

Among the fruits recommended for bearded dragons are:

- Berries of most varieties
- Chopped apples
- Chopped pears

A small amount of finely chopped tender baby spinach leaves can be added to the diet of developing bearded dragons to provide additional iron. Spinach, broccoli, and other cruciferous vegetables should be fed in very small amounts no more than once a week. Too much of these foods can be harmful to your beardies. You can round out the diet by adding chopped, frozen mixed vegetables that have been thawed.

Various lettuces (iceberg, romaine, bib, Boston, and red or green leaf) should not be fed except in an emergency. Beardies love such lettuces, but they hold little nutritional value for them. If you must feed lettuce, it should be amply supplemented with sprinkled calcium or other vitamin and mineral supplements made for reptiles.

Commercial Lizard Foods

A number of manufacturers have developed pelleted foods that can be fed to beardies out of the jar. These prepared foods can be blended with regular vegetable diets. Some beardie keepers report that their bearded dragons gobble up pellets, while others find that they refuse them and some even spit them out if they eat them by accident! To date, I have not been able to get any bearded dragon to eat a commercial food without combining it with something else.

If you coach your bearded dragon to eat these foods without resorting to this kind of trickery, it is still important that you don't rely on commercial foods to the exclusion of other dietary items. At this time, there are no long-term published studies indicating that commercial foods are adequate or superior as a sole source of nutrition for bearded dragons.

Insects

Bearded dragons will eat a wide variety of insects. If you catch the insects yourself, you must be absolutely certain they haven't been exposed to any insecticides, herbicides, or chemical fertilizers. Most insects suitable for feeding to

Commercial lizard foods can provide good nutrition (if your beardie will eat them), but they must be part of a diet that includes fresh fruit and vegetables.

lizards can be purchased commercially, so you know they are chemical-free. A list of some suppliers is included in the appendix. Pet supply stores, particularly those that sell reptiles, also stock suitable feeder insects.

You should feed the insects a highly nutritional dietary supplement before feeding them to your beardies. This is a simple process known as "gut loading." The insect becomes a carrier of the nutrients that it has consumed. Crickets, mealworms, and small mice can be fed a diet of high-quality rodent chow. Crickets, a favorite of bearded dragons, can also be fed or dusted with one of the commercially prepared high-calcium and vitamin D3 cricket supplements. Pellets designed to feed lizards also make a good gut-loader food for crickets. Place a handful of the pellets in a jar cap, spray them lightly with water, and soon your feeder crickets will be all over them. Vitamin C is provided by giving your crickets some sliced oranges; this also gives them fluids and eliminates the need for a messy watering sponge. Avoid putting a water dish in your crickets' housing, as the crickets fall in, swim around, and then quickly drown.

Gut-loaded insects should be fed to your bearded dragons as soon as possible after they've been fed their enriched diet. If you delay, the insects will pass the nutrients before your beardie has a chance to gobble them up.

Crickets are a great beardie food. First feed the crickets well, and your lizard will get all the nutrition that's in the insects.

Feeding Babies— Newborn to 4 Months Old

You have to be careful about overfeeding baby beardies. Although their growth is rapid during this time and they need plenty of food, like babies of all species they need to have smaller meals and to be fed more frequently than their adult counterparts.

Baby beardies have hearty appetites. A baby beardie would not hesitate, for example, to attempt to overpower and eat an adult cricket. However, the result could be disastrous for your lizard. Its small digestive system is apt to become injured by the tougher parts of the cricket (such as the serrated legs). Moreover, should it manage to stuff such a morsel into its mouth, the large bulk of the food in the beardie's stomach could put pressure on the nerves in the lower part of the lizard's body, causing temporary, or worse, permanent rear leg paralysis. Therefore, you need to feed baby beardies crickets that are only a few weeks old or no larger than half an inch long. Cricket suppliers grade their crickets using a numbering system, and sell all sizes. Newborn crickets are known as "pinheads."

This baby cricket is just the right size for this 1-week-old beardie. The penny gives you an idea of how small they both are.

If you're feeding mealworm larvae to baby beardies, select smaller, just-molted specimens. Just-molted mealworms are creamy white, whereas larvae with tougher, chitinous shells are yellow or brownish-yellow. This tough exterior is difficult for baby beardies to digest and can easily cause a gastrointestinal blockage that could be fatal.

Another good, tender choice for baby beardies is the larvae of the waxmoth. These are relatively small, and they are so soft that they are not a problem to digest.

Baby bearded dragons should be fed only three or four pinhead or baby crickets, or two or three small freshly molted mealworms or waxmoth larvae per meal.

It is also important to gut-load all insects and dust them two or three times a week with specially formulated reptile vitamin and mineral supplement powders. Some of these are fine enough to stick on the insect for several minutes while they are being offered to your beardie.

At least one breeder reports that he has had unusually good luck feeding newborn beardies termites, although they are difficult to find (he raises his own by burying a rotten piece of wood out in the backyard). He makes sure each baby beardie gets a few termites daily and claims that he has never lost a hatchling due to failure to thrive.

Feed Baby Beardies Frequently

I noted in chapter 6 that if you need to go away for a day or two, your beardies can be left food and water and will still be in good shape when you return. After three days, adults must be fed again. However, this is not the case with baby beardies; babies need to be fed twice a day (at a minimum) during their first six months of life. You cannot escape the daily chore of feeding baby beardies without impairing their development or worse yet, seeing them die. Therefore, if you must be away from home, either bring them with you (in a small plastic carrier or terrarium), or be sure a trusted friend or relative will take up your feeding chores when you are absent.

Conventional wisdom holds that during this developmental stage, beardies need a significant amount of animal protein. Be that as it may, don't hesitate to offer them vegetables and get them started early on a healthy diet. Vegetable matter should be finely chopped with a food chopper or a sharp knife and offered in small quantities in a tiny dish (a large bottle cap works nicely). Direct the beardie's nose to the dish and then leave it alone and allow it to discover a taste for veggies. A veggie meal should be offered every other day at this stage.

Feeding Adults— 4 Months to Adulthood

Once your beardies are around 4 months old, feed them at least twice a day. Veggies should be offered every other meal and the young beardies should get a supplement every day.

At 8 months to full adulthood (at about 1 year, or when they are 8 to 10 inches long), they should still be fed at least once every 12 hours, and should be eating greens at least once every day and animal protein around two or three times a week—as much as they want until they stop eating. It is helpful if you douse the vegetable matter with a little extra water. This is a good way to get fluids into your beardies, and it will be appreciated. You can supplement the insects or veggies with vitamin and mineral powders every other day, and scale back to once every other day when full adulthood is reached. Note, however, that breeding females need extra nutrients for embryo, yolk, and eggshell formation (see chapter 9).

Adult beardies should be fed at least once a day—preferably twice. Feed coarsely chopped or unchopped greens and mixed fruits and veggies daily. Feeding basically means placing a quantity of the selected food in the cage where they can nibble on it all day. Vegetable matter should be removed when it becomes dried out.

Adults can be fed crickets that are 6 weeks old or older, larger mealworms, and king mealworms (*Zoophobas morio*, or "zoophobias" as they are commonly known). Waxmoth larvae (also known as

All kinds of worms make good foods. Avoid insects with hard shells, such as beetles.

waxworms) and other bugs may also be fed. Avoid hard-shelled beetles, as they can cause intestinal blockage. Pinky (newborn) mice and fuzzy mice can also be eaten by young adults, and larger adult beardies will even subdue and eat young live mice. These animal foods should be fed only once every two or three days. Adults don't really need supplements, but you should still gut-load their insects. And weekly supplements will not do any harm. Adults will eat any amount of insects until they are no longer hungry. The only danger with overfeeding adult beardies is obesity.

Variety Is Important

It is important to feed a variety of foods and to offer as many as possible—do not become dependent on just one type of food. Vegetables should be the main component of your beardie's diet. Although beardies will relish young mice, they are high in fat and your beardies run the risk of becoming obese as a result of a steady diet of such foods.

Just like us, beardies thrive on a varied diet. Vegetables should be the main component on your pet's menu.

As dietary generalists, bearded dragons have been known to eat small birds, eggs, and fish. A willingness to eat fish is surprising, as most bearded dragons live in areas with little or no water, let alone large stocks of small fish they are capable of catching. In captivity, this is a different matter. Feeder fish or even pieces of fish you might buy for yourself can be placed in a shallow dish of water and the beardies will readily gobble them up. Fish is high in nutrients and is a good occasional change of diet for beardies. However, tropical fish may pose a danger. Tropical fish often harbor a parasite called *Microspora* that bearded dragons can contract. There is no treatment to rid fish or beardies of this parasite, and the disease can be fatal.

Supplements

There is a bewildering array of vitamin and mineral supplements on the market for reptiles, so it's often necessary to put on those reading glasses and take a long, hard look at ingredient lists. Avoid products that don't list the ingredients on the package. For calcium and vitamin D3 supplementation, many experienced beardie lovers use a triple calcium product (with no vitamin A or other vitamins or minerals).

Although there are some excellent supplements available, your beardies should get nearly all the vitamins and proteins they need from a varied diet of animal and vegetable matter. For baby and juvenile beardies, though, supplements should be added to one feeding every day. When your beardies reach a length of 8 to 10 inches, their growth will slow down and you can begin supplementing their diet every other day.

Once adulthood is reached, the lizards are at their full size and supplements can be added weekly. Breeding females should receive supplements every day or every other day until two weeks after egg-laying. If you expect to breed a particular female several times in one season, you should supplement her diet daily.

Water for Your Beardies

Water is essential to life everywhere. Reptiles and amphibians that live in areas where there is little or no rainfall, and in the absence of surface ground water, adapt by conserving what water they can from their food and excreting their urine in either a solid or semisolid state along with their feces.

The Water Dish

The traditional way of offering water is to provide your lizards with a water dish. Such a dish can be bought in a pet supply shop in decorative styles, or you can use any shallow glass dish or even an upside-down jar lid or bottle cap. Be sure the water in the dish isn't too deep, or your pets could drown. Not all beardies drink from water dishes, so you must make sure that they are using it for this purpose. Some beardies will use their water dishes as a toilet (the dish must be cleaned right away when this occurs). Often, beardies will throw substrate into their dish as they wander through it.

Clearly, water dishes tend to get fouled quickly and they must be kept scrupulously clean—if not, they will soon turn into a dangerous source of

Some beardie owners let their pet swim the bathtub now and then. The water should be warm but not hot. Beardies will drink the water in the tub, and likely will also eliminate in it—so be sure to disinfect the tub after a swim.

> ## Water Dish Tip
>
> If you are intent on getting your beardie to drink from a water dish, you might try giving your pet a noncarbonated, lightly perfumed or flavored water. When I offered regular bottled spa water, one of my beardies refused to drink, but when I offered water lightly scented with strawberry flavoring, he lapped it up. After a few "fill-ups," I replaced the scented water with plain spa water and this beardie has been drinking from the water dish ever since! Sneaky, eh?
>
> If you are worried about the contents of commercial "designer" waters, make your own by squeezing the juice of a berry into the water. Chilling before serving is optional.

bacterial and fungal contamination. Beardies may have low levels of bacteria in their feces that will concentrate and bloom in water dishes. By drinking water thus contaminated, the lizards will obtain higher doses of enteric bacteria that could result in diarrhea, other gastrointestinal problems, or even in their death. Such germs may also be transmitted to people. It is very important, therefore, to make sure that water dishes are kept absolutely spotless at all times. Handle dirty dishes with care, washing, disinfecting, and rinsing them well in very hot water in a sink that is not used for food preparation or human dish and utensil washing.

If your local tap water does not taste good, or if you would not drink it yourself, be sure to give bottled spring or noncarbonated mineral water to your beardies. The trace elements in such waters will be beneficial to your pets, and you will not risk harming them with local tap or well water. Distilled or purified waters are devoid of such elements, and while they are good to put in your car battery, they offer no benefit to your beardies but will do in a pinch.

Sprinkling the Greens

If you cannot coach your beardie to drink from a water dish, it is best to dispense with it and rely on watering down the vegetables and fruits you feed, or spraying as a means of getting water into your lizard. Mist the plant matter with

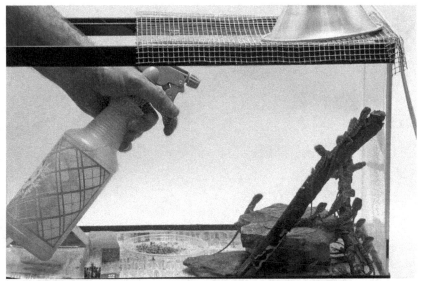

Lightly misting your beardies several times a day is a very natural way to give them water. This tank is full of babies.

a thin layer of water and your pets will obtain much needed fluid just by eating it. Animal foods also contain fluids that are passed on to beardies.

In addition to using food as a water vehicle, you can also lightly mist your beardies several times a day with a plant sprayer. It's very similar to the way they would get it in the wild—dripping from leaves and trees or from morning dew. For the health of your beardies, buy a new spray bottle to be used just for this purpose and do not use it for anything else. In their arid environment, bearded beardies will lap up rainwater as it drips down their heads toward their mouth. Like frogs, beardies love rain and enjoy being sprinkled this way.

Chapter 8

Keeping Your Beardie Healthy

Because it is illegal to export wild-caught animals from Australia, all bearded dragons in the hobbyist or pet trade today are captive-bred. As a result, the lizards tend to be healthy and hardy. Lizards that live in the wild acquire all sorts of bacterial, fungal, and parasitic diseases to which they develop immunities. When these wild animals are caught, shipped, and kept in captivity, these animals become stressed and their immunity rapidly declines. Hobbyists, in turn, wind up with sick animals—some overtly so.

Nonetheless, even captive-born beardies can contract a variety of diseases. They can acquire them in large-scale holding and breeding facilities where handlers go from one lizard to another without washing their hands. They may also become ill if such handlers do not take other appropriate precautions, such as removing water or food dishes and then returning them to other tanks without first disinfecting them. Many respiratory infections may be airborne, so beardies can become ill just by being in close proximity to other lizards who are sick.

Choosing a Veterinarian

It is important to find a veterinarian with experience treating reptiles when you first obtain your bearded dragon. Don't wait until your pet is under the weather to locate a qualified professional. When considering prospective vets in your area, you should ask them if they have experience with reptiles. While most vets are well trained in small animal care, only a few have had any training in the unique medical requirements of reptiles.

How Do You Know Your Beardie Is Sick?

Sick bearded dragons behave like sick puppies, kittens, and, yes, even people. They look sick, they act sick and they show symptoms suggestive of the kind of illness that is affecting them. If your beardie is sluggish or won't eat, if it lies flat on the ground (a posture that is normal for sleeping at night but not when the animal is awake during the day), if it doesn't move much or at all, or if your beardie's natural color seems faded and pale, take your beardie to the veterinarian immediately.

The Association of Reptile and Amphibian Veterinarians (listed in the appendix) can help you find a veterinarian in your area. You can also find veterinarians who are qualified to work with reptiles by calling your local herpetological society. Doctors with no experience with lizards can make an uninformed decision that may cost a lot of money as well as the life of your animal.

Some of the illnesses listed in this chapter can be treated first at home—if the animal is still in the very early stages of the disease. But if you can see no improvement within a few days of home treatment, it is best to take your beardie in for a veterinary examination. Make sure the proposed treatment will actually benefit your beardie.

Hereditary Diseases

Hereditary or genetic diseases are problems that bearded dragons are born with. They are more commonly found in the offspring of bearded dragons that are close relatives. For example, when one parent is the sibling of the other, it is more likely that a genetic disorder will occur in the children than if the parents are unrelated. To take an extreme and amusing example, if a family of bearded dragons has weak eyesight and two closely related members are bred with each other, it is possible that your bearded dragon will need eyeglasses to see its food.

One class of hereditary diseases involves bearded dragons born with tail and limb deformities, some of which are ultimately lethal. In one recent case, a beardie was born live with one head and two bodies. It died not long after hatching. As a rule, egg abnormalities such as this result in the birth of either

Hereditary diseases are more common in the off-spring of parents who are close relatives.

Siamese twins (two fully formed but connected lizards) or one lizard with two heads. Scientists are not certain if such deformities are truly hereditary, if they are based on improper egg husbandry, or if they result from a combination of both. A genetic basis for these deformities is supported by the fact that other hatchlings from the same clutch, incubated in just the same way, are perfectly normal.

Although many reptiles become ill with cancerous diseases and tumors, to date this has not been a problem with bearded dragons. However, if there is a genetic basis for the predisposition to such diseases, and immunity to them is diminished by inbreeding, such disorders may be seen in the future, because more and more beardies in the current captive-bred market tend to be related in one way or another. This kind of situation is engendered by the absence of new, foreign, or wild-caught stock that would add greater variety to the gene pool. There appears to be enough unrelated or very distantly related breeding stock available, so this is not likely to occur any time soon. But unless new stock is made available, there will come a day in the United States when every bearded dragon is related to every other bearded dragon in some way.

Nutritional Disorders

All reptiles and amphibians, including bearded dragons, are subject to a number of nutritional disorders.

Calcium and Vitamin D3 Deficiencies

Calcium and vitamin D3 deficiencies are very problematic for beardies. Acute calcium deficiency produces convulsive twitching, spasms, "the shakes," and full-blown seizures that can and often do result in death. On a more subtle level,

Adequate calcium is especially critical for growing babies and breeding females.

occurring over time, deficiencies in calcium and vitamin D3 result in poor bone growth, brittleness of existing bones, and soft bones (known as "rubber jaw"). These can result in stunted growth, deformities of long bones and, when the jaw is affected, they can impair or prevent feeding.

Preventing and treating calcium and vitamin D3 deficiencies involve exposing the lizard to direct, unfiltered sunlight for several hours each day, plus adding a dietary supplement to the food consisting of calcium carbonate, calcium gluconate, and vitamin D3 (sometimes called triple calcium). Note that a beardie's intake of phosphorus is also important, because phosphorus interacts with calcium in the diet. As part of the beardie's diet, phosphorus should ideally be present in amounts equal to half that of the useable calcium. Phosphorus levels that exceed calcium levels can prevent proper absorption of calcium for bone growth.

It is critical to provide a balanced nutritionally adequate or calcium-supplemented diet, particularly for developing juvenile or baby lizards, as well as adult females being bred. Failure to do so can result in rickets, metabolic bone disease, impaired nervous system transmission, and poor eggshell production. Calcium is also important for normal cardiac function and is an integral part of healthy skin, bone, muscle, and blood. Regular exposure to full-spectrum lighting, plus a healthy, balanced diet, will head off any deficiencies.

The Ramifications of Hostility Among Beardies

The aggressive nature of beardies with other beardies and the resulting injuries make large-scale rearing of clutches in a single enclosure a serious problem. Buyers only want perfect specimens, and in order to provide them, baby beardies need to be housed separately. This is obviously more expensive and more labor-intensive than housing and feeding a large number of animals in a communal enclosure.

The need to keep beardies in separate cages is one reason why the wholesale cost of baby bearded dragons is likely to be ten times the wholesale price of a baby green iguana, which can be communally raised. With so much going for them, bearded dragons are definitely worth the extra money, though.

naked eye, but the organisms that cause bacterial and viral diseases are so small they cannot be seen without a microscope—although their symptoms are usually easy to spot.

The common feature among all infectious diseases is that they can be transmitted between the environment and the host (in this case, your bearded dragon is the host), or from one animal to another. On occasion, such diseases can be transmitted from animals to people and vice versa.

Respiratory Infections

Respiratory ailments can be caused by bacteria, viruses, or fungi. They are rare among beardies. When they do occur, they are often the result of improper environmental conditions, including temperatures that are too low, humidity levels that are too high, or both. Symptoms include gaping, noisy breathing, puffiness around the throat pouch, and mucus discharge from the nostrils and/or mouth.

Because such infections are potentially fatal, a trip to the veterinarian is necessary. In the meantime, keep your sick beardie warm (in an enclosure that is 90°F) and at a relatively low humidity.

Note, however, that gaping may also be the result of overheating, something that should be obvious if you check the temperature of the enclosure. Gaping may also be a symptom of lung worms, a parasitic disease. If you are at

Respiratory infections are rare in beardies and are usually the result of poor husbandry. If you keep your beardie's home clean, warm, and dry, this shouldn't be a problem.

all uncertain about the cause of your beardie's distress, make an appointment with your veterinarian right away.

Gastrointestinal Infections

Gastrointestinal infections are most commonly caused by an overgrowth of bacteria such as *E. coli, Salmonella sp., Pseudomonas sp.,* or other organisms. Symptoms include loss of appetite, weight loss, listlessness, and foul-smelling diarrhea. Lizards do not vomit, so even if they have symptoms of nausea they cannot relieve themselves in this way. A gastrointestinal infection should be evaluated quickly by a veterinarian, who can do a fecal examination. Delay can be fatal, so consider this type of infection a real emergency.

Viral Infections

Recently, adenoviruses have emerged as one of the most likely causes of viral disease in beardies. Adenoviruses are members of the family Adenoviridae, and more than forty different types are known to infect people, causing upper respiratory tract, gastrointestinal, and even eye infections. In beardies they cause enteritis with diarrhea, which may lead to severe liver damage and death.

If you suspect adenovirus in your beardie, you should see a veterinarian. Because antibiotics are ineffective for fighting viral infections, there is no easy cure. The best treatment is to warm the animal, inducing a low-grade fever that is unfavorable to the virus (see the box on page 101).

Antibiotics may be required to fight secondary bacterial infections in animals with adenovirus infection. Experts believe that bearded dragons and perhaps other lizards with this disease are infected by a strain of adenovirus that selectively only affects them and not people.

Other lizard viruses known to occur are from the family of pox-viruses and *Papilloma* (herpes) virus. Papillomas, or flattened "warts," were discovered in emerald lizards, at the base of the tail in females and at the base of the neck in males. The warts are associated with mating bites. As part of the mating ritual, females bite males on the neck and males bite females at the base of the tail. Because bearded dragons are also known to bite one another during mating, it is possible that they may develop similar viral infections.

Biting is part of the mating ritual in beardies. Viral infections may develop at the site of these bites.

Fungal Infections

Fungal diseases occur in damp, warm environments and thus are not a known problem in bearded dragons, who dwell in arid areas. Some types of cage substrate, such as corncob (which is heavily infused with dormant fungal spores), rapidly vegetate with fungal growth when exposed to dampness and heat. Corncob-based substrates should not be used for beardies or most other reptiles for this reason. This type of substrate is also not recommended for any reptile that may accidentally ingest it with food matter. This can result in intestinal blockage.

In beardies, the most likely place a fungus would occur is in a skin abrasion or a cut. This should be quickly treated with an antifungal ointment, such as Lotrimin, or by a veterinarian using an antifungal agent or an antibiotic known to fight fungal conditions.

Fighting Infections at Home

In some cases, you may be able to treat infections by increasing the temperature of your beardie's basking spot up to between 95°F and 100°F. Be careful not to cook your beardie, however. In nature, reptiles with infections tend to allow themselves to heat up, inducing a fever, if you will, in an apparent effort to subdue or kill off infectious organisms. According to some breeders and hobbyists, this simple home treatment frequently works better than expensive antibiotics. If your beardie does not seem to be feeling better the next day, though, it needs to see a veterinarian.

Parasitic Infections

Parasites are also infectious. They may be either microscopic (protozoan or unicellular parasites) or large enough to see with the naked eye (metazoan or multicellular parasites). Parasites are classified by their physical relationship with their host. Those that live on the outside of a host are known as ectoparasites. Those that live inside a host are called endoparasites.

Reptiles may harbor both types of parasites. There are many ways to rid your beardies of parasites, and not all of them can be addressed here. As a rule, it is best to seek professional help when your lizard has a parasitic infection. Many hobbyists, however, effectively use home treatments on their animals. This is only a good solution if you are confident that you can diagnose the problem properly and treat it competently.

Ectoparasites

Mites, fleas, ticks, and maggots are among the ectoparasites that might plague your beardie. Hobbyists treat ectoparasites with No-Pest Strips placed not far from (but not in or on top of) cages, hoping to attract mites and ticks off the animal and kill them with the vapors in the strip. Other methods include bathing the animal in dilute solutions of Betadine and water (colored like weak tea) or a solution of original Listerine and water (tinged light gold).

Some hobbyists use a topical solution of the antiparasite drug Ivermectin, which is available over-the-counter in animal feed stores. Recommended doses of this drug are provided for huge animals—horses and cows. It should be diluted for use as a topical application at a ratio of 0.5 ml of the drug to a quart of water. Using the drug internally can be very dangerous to your animal, so this should be left to a knowledgeable veterinarian.

> **T I P**
>
> If you observe your beardie becoming lethargic and inactive for no apparent reason, as a precaution you should have your veterinarian do a fecal check just to make sure your dragon's lethargy isn't due to a parasitic infection.

There is very little you can do to prevent fleas, ticks, and mites from attacking your bearded dragon if they are in your home or come in on other pets. When you see such blood-sucking ectoparasites on your lizard, isolate the animal and take it to the veterinarian as soon as possible. There are some strategies to kill such parasites before they infect your lizard, such as placing a flea collar or fly paper in the vicinity of your beardie enclosure, and these may be worth a try. But you must be careful not to harm your animal with these products, as they may contain volatile, toxic substances. Your veterinarian will be your best guide here.

When you pick your beardie up, eventually let it settle on your chest, but keep a supporting hand nearby.

Keep Yourself Healthy, Too

One of the most common (and normal) intestinal bacteria in reptiles is *Salmonella*. *Salmonella*, along with a variety of other microorganisms, are known as zoonotic diseases, or zoonoses. Zoonoses are infections that can be transmitted from animals to humans, and vice versa.

Salmonella, and in fact, most zoonoses, are entirely preventable by thoroughly washing your hands for thirty seconds with hot water and disinfectant soap after handling any reptiles. In addition, you must be careful when cleaning your reptile's cage furnishings and water bowls in sinks used for human activities, such as kitchen sinks and bathroom sinks. Be sure to remove all articles used for human purposes from the sink area, and to thoroughly disinfect sinks and countertops as soon as you are finished. If possible, devote one sink in your home for beardie use only.

Zoonoses are especially dangerous to people who are immunocompromised because of a disease, such as HIV, or a medication, or other treatment they are receiving. Children under 8 years old are liable to suffer more seriously from zoonotic infection than are older children and adults. Fetuses are also at high risk, and accordingly, moms-to-be must be meticulous when handling reptiles or cleaning cages, or leave the chores to others.

Endoparasites

Cryptosporidosis

One of the most prevalent endoparasites found in bearded dragons in the United States is a coccidian (a single-celled organism) known as *Cryptosporidium*, which causes a disease called cryptosporidosis, or "crypto" for short. In recent years, crypto has been showing up in some municipal water supplies, and it is not clear whether it is resistant to conventional chlorination procedures or if the water supplies in question are being adequately treated. The organism is too small to be captured by many home and industrial water filtering systems. Boiling tap water or providing bottled water are alternatives in areas where crypto is known to be present in the water supply.

Veterinary researchers have reported finding crypto in increasing numbers among captive reptiles, often wiping out entire collections before its presence was detected and could be properly treated. Breeders may start out shipping apparently healthy animals that then become stressed by the rigors of transport and handling. By the time they reach the home hobbyist's cage, their previously undetectable infection may be a full-blown case. Such animals need to be diagnosed and treated by a veterinarian, but if the infection is overwhelming the prognosis may not be good. They can also pass the infection to other beardies.

Coccidiosis

Another coccidian commonly found in bearded dragons is *Isospora amphiboluri*, which causes the disease coccidiosis. This organism, in fact, is named after an earlier (discarded) genus name for beardies—*Amphibolurus*. These parasites are so common that they may be considered commensals—microorganisms that do not harm their host. However, it is not a good idea to leave them untreated in captive animals, which may have depressed immune systems as a result of inadequate conditions or the mere stress of captivity. In beardies of questionable health, these organisms can rapidly reproduce and reach excessive and definitely harmful levels.

A kiss is not just a kiss. Reptiles carry Salmonella and other bacteria that can make us sick. Protect yourself by washing up with soap and hot water after handling your beardie.

Isospora invade the mucus lining of the intestinal tract, which they feed on in order to grow and reproduce. In heavy infestations, they can cause your beardie stomach pain, diarrhea, and nutritional malabsorption. Moreover, in connection with the diarrhea, beardies lose fluids (which they can ill afford, given the difficulty hobbyists have in getting them to accept fluids at all). Needless to say, this situation can easily lead to your lizard's death.

Because it is not known where or how coccidiosis is contracted, getting and isolating a newborn beardie is no guarantee it will be *Isospora*-free. Some veterinarians have suggested it may be passed to unborn beardies before the embryo is encased in its shell, or it may even migrate through the shell wall.

There are only two drugs available that may work to combat coccidiosis: sulfamethoxine and trimethoprim-sulfa. Sulfa drugs should be used only if coccidiosis is a confirmed diagnosis, according to veterinary authorities on these parasites. Because the bug will come back as fast as you eliminate it, you also have to change cages frequently during the treatment cycle to prevent re-infection. Infected animals should actually have two cages: one for housing the beardie and one to be sterilized. The animal should be moved back and forth into a freshly sterilized cage frequently. You may have to keep this process up for as long as six weeks before your veterinarian gives your beardie a clean bill of health. It is best to keep the cages free of accessories—everything in the cage will also have to be sterilized repeatedly.

Don't put your beardie on a high perch, because it could jump off and be injured. These are semi-arboreal animals—they don't climb all the way up trees.

Handling Do's and Don'ts

Babies and Juveniles

- Don't suddenly grab your bearded dragon.
- Don't grab them by their tails or limbs.
- Do approach them slowly, gently, and without threatening gestures.
- Do place your finger under the chin and extend it under the body; the baby will hold onto your finger.
- Do transfer babies and their support to your hand.
- Do always fully support your bearded dragon in the palm of your hand. Its head should be facing away from you.
- Don't squeeze or press on your baby dragon. Children must be especially cautioned, supervised, and taught not to do this.
- If your beardie decides to make a run for it or starts getting restless, don't suddenly grab it or make a fist to restrain it. Keep the palm of your other hand open or flat and slightly cupped and quickly put it over your lizard, making a "cave" for it. Beardies love to hide, even if it's in a human hand.

Adults

- Do approach and pick up your lizard by first supporting the body.
- Don't grab or catch your beardie by a leg or by grabbing its tail.
- Do hold it in your hand and support its tail with your upper arm.
- Do gradually allow your beardie to perch on your chest or shoulder, but keep a supporting hand handy, because adults tend not to hang on as tightly as babies.
- Don't place them in situations where they might be tempted to jump from high places, because they can break limbs or toes or otherwise injure themselves. Beardies don't lives in trees; they normally perch on bushes, rock formations, and fence rails rarely more than few feet high.

Microsporiodosis

Another endoparasite found in bearded dragons is *Microspora sp.*, which causes microsporiodosis. Until recently, *Microspora sp.* was believed to predominantly infect fish, most notably ornamental tropical fish. It has rarely been identified in amphibians and some reptiles, and only quite recently in beardies. Tropical fish hobbyists have much experience with this parasite and admit there is no defini-

- Do shamelessly bribe bearded dragons to come to you by offering their favorite food from your hand; soon they begin to associate being handled with getting goodies to eat. This also works for dogs and horses and most other companion animals.

If you need to transport your beardie to the vet or take it out to a show, it is best to carry your pet in a suitably sized carry cage. Since beardies love to hide, the last thing you want is for your lizard to lodge itself under the front seat of your car and not come out. If you use public transportation, your fellow passengers may not be lizard lovers and they will appreciate you keeping your pet in a carrying cage.

Although claws are not much of a problem in babies and juveniles, adult beardies develop sharp claws that can scratch up your hands and arms. These wounds may even contain traces of beardie fecal material, so they need to be disinfected. You can trim your beardie's claws with a cat claw trimmer, clipping only the sharp blackened tips. If you clip too much, you risk cutting a vein and your beardie will bleed and feel pain. Since beardies have claws to help them perch, some beardie fanciers prefer wearing a long-sleeved shirt and smooth leather gloves and leaving their claws intact. If you feel you must clip your beardie's nails you may want to let the vet do it.

And, as has been emphasized elsewhere in this book, always wash and/or disinfect your hands thoroughly after handling your lizard, or any reptile or amphibian pet. This applies to grown-ups and (especially) kids handling these animals. Beardies may pick up bacteria on their skin from their tank that, while harmless to them, can cause problems in humans. There are several good hand disinfectants available in stores that will prevent the risk of catching any nasty bugs from your pet lizards.

Always be sure to disinfect any scratches a beardie might unintentionally make. And while beardies almost never bite, if they do, such wounds should also be thoroughly washed and disinfected. If they become reddened or sore and painful, see your doctor.

tive treatment for it. In fish, the organism not only occupies the gastrointestinal tract, but it also attacks internal organs and eventually kills its host.

In view of the appearance of this organism in bearded dragons, it may be unwise to offer them feeder tropical fish that you might purchase in an aquarium store. *Microspora* cause problems for bearded dragons, and any animal they infect, for two very important reasons: They have a direct life cycle (they don't

need an intermediate host to reproduce), and they form highly resistant
spores that can exist up to a year or
more in the environment, even in
the absence of a host. Some researchers believe the source of infection in
beardies may, indeed, be ingestion
of such spores, which are liable to be
anywhere.

Amoebic Dysentery

Another dangerous parasite, which
is rare in the U.S. water supply (but
not in some other countries where
sewerage and sanitation may be poor), is *Entamoeba invadens*. This organism
causes amoebic dysentery, which is not very different from the same condition
in humans caused by *Entamoeba histolytica*. The parasite causes gastroenteritis
marked by bloody diarrhea and failure or unwillingness to eat (anorexia). It
often culminates in death. It can be treated by a veterinarian once the diagnosis
is established.

Pinworms

Beardies are frequently afflicted
by infestations of pinworms, also
known as oxyurids. Generally, pinworms are less harmful and easier to
treat than other parasites. However,
they can quickly reach troublesome
levels. Your veterinarian can check
for pinworms by examining your
beardie's feces; they are treated with
a short course of the drug Panacur.

*Your beardie relies on you for care. If you notice any
changes in behavior, call your reptile veterinarian.*

Dystocia

The most common reproductive disorder seen in female adult beardies is egg-binding or dystocia. There are many possible causes for egg-binding, including poor diet and calcium deficiency, generalized weakness or debilitation, low weight, obesity, and other illness. If your beardie cannot find or select a suitable site to dig a nest, the stress can also result in egg-binding.

If the cause is anything but the last (which you can rectify by quickly establishing a deep soil-based substrate for the beardie to build her nest), then a trip to the veterinarian is in order as soon as the problem is recognized. A drug known as pitocin or vasotocin can be administered, which will induce contractions that lead to the expulsion of the eggs. Egg-binding can be fatal if not quickly relieved. If the lizard does not respond to the drug, surgery to remove the eggs may be necessary.

Observe a gravid female carefully. If your beardie is egg-bound, you want to be aware of it as soon as the problem arises. If the animal stops eating for several days and is constantly rooting about looking to deposit her eggs but is either unable to do so or is unable to select a suitable site (even if you have provided one), then you can be reasonably certain your beardie is in trouble.

Neurological Disorders

Most neurological problems seen in bearded dragons can be traced to a dietary deficiency. It is particularly important to be sure your beardies get enough calcium, as a diet lacking in calcium may lead to neurological symptoms, such as spasms, twitching, and seizures.

Lizard owners should also be on the lookout for inclusion body disease (IBD), an unidentified virus that attacks the brain and spinal tissues. Although infection with this disease has not yet been found in beardies, it has been well-documented in snakes and is believed to have spread to captive lizards. Symptoms include "star-gazing" (an upward tilt of the head) and other strange postures maintained over long periods.

There is no known cure for this condition, but early recognition is essential to limit the spread of the disease in collections. Affected animals should be quarantined, preferably in separate rooms. After coming into contact with an affected animal, thoroughly disinfect your hands and even change your clothing before having any contact with healthy lizards.

Environmental Toxins

A wide variety of common household substances can be toxic to amphibians and reptiles, including bearded dragons. These include glass cleaners and other cleaning compounds, insecticides, chemical fertilizers, weed killers, and perhaps even the disinfectant soap that you use to clean your animal's food or water dishes. Such substances need to be kept far away from your beardies.

When cleaning food and water dishes, be sure to thoroughly rinse away any soapy or disinfectant residue. Be especially careful about using insecticide sprays or other volatile compounds around your beardies—the molecules of these sprays enter the air freely and can be inhaled by your lizard. Exposure to chemicals can result in neurological problems, with a variety of symptoms, such as seizures, twitching, the stargazing symptom, and other bizarre and unusual signs.

If you have live plants in your enclosure, remember that beardies like to eat leaves and the leaves of many ornamental houseplants may be toxic. In addition, store-bought plants may have been sprayed with pesticides or a chemical to make the leaves shiny. Be sure to wash these plants thoroughly before placing them in your beardie's cage. Artificial plants are a far better choice.

Our environment is full of substances that can be toxic to beardies. Keep them far away from your pet.

Baby beardies should not brumate. They need all their time to grow.

Brumation

As we mentioned in chapter 2, brumation is a period of inactivity and even lethargy that may be dictated by a combination of shortened days, extremes of temperature, and a beardie's natural predilection to become lethargic and inactive whenever conditions are not just right. If your beardie doesn't naturally brumate, there is no reason to force it to do so. And baby beardies, those less than a year or so old, should never be forced to brumate, because this is a prime period for growth and development that shouldn't be needlessly interrupted.

If your beardie does brumate, here some tips for keeping it healthy:

- Keep a basking light on 8 to 10 hours a day.
- Reduce the ambient cage temperature to 65°F to 70°F.
- Provide a normal basking place, since a brumating beardie may decide to eat but won't be able to digest food without warmth.
- Continue to offer food during this period, because you never know when a brumating beardie might suddenly become active and want a meal.

Chapter 9

Breeding Bearded Dragons

According to some longtime professional bearded dragon breeders, the huge numbers of these lizards being bred in captivity outside of Australia may soon make them the most popular species of pet lizard. In spite of a paucity of field research on beardies in the wild, their captive husbandry and breeding is now among the best understood and managed of any agamid lizard.

Sexing

The first consideration for any would-be breeder is to be sure to place a male and a female together. Two males may soon start fighting and hurt each other before they can be separated. Even males and females play rough, with males biting females on the neck and females taking nips at the toes and tail tips of the males.

In bearded dragons, there are a number of ways to distinguish males from females, even though they display no obvious differences in color, structure, or external anatomy. However, males have larger heads than females and bob their heads more slowly. Females tend to be larger in the abdominal girth than males. The gular or "beard" region tends to be darker in males than in females. Males have larger, more prominent pores around their anal and femoral region. The femoral pores of bearded dragons are not located in the middle of a scale, but are actually between two scales.

When you place them side by side, the difference between males and females is easier to see. The male (on the left) has a larger head than the female. The beard also tends to be darker in males.

If an experienced hobbyist or breeder shows you how, you can also evert the hemipenes (the pair of male reproductive organs), thus identifying the specimen in hand as a male. But the best way to separate the sexes is by looking at the hemipenile bulges, which are located on each side of the base of the tail. To make these bulges appear, place an 8-month to 1-year-old or older lizard (6 to 8 inches long, from snout to vent) flat on its stomach and, holding it flat with one hand along the back, use the other hand to gently lift the tail so the tail is almost straight up at a 90-degree angle from the body. Be careful not to bend back the tail too far or you might snap a vertebra at the base of the tail. If you see two bulges on either side of the tail base, then you have a male. If you see one bulge more centrally located, the beardie is a female.

Conditioning and Nutrition

Once you have identified an opposite-sex pair, you must get them ready for the big event. Before mating is attempted, it is essential that you house males and females separately and keep them well fed on a varied diet. For two or three weeks before mating, add a triple calcium supplement to the female's diet every day. This contributes to the more efficient formation of the egg shell.

A number of factors influence breeding, including temperature and cycles of light and darkness. In the premating period, your beardies should get ten hours of light per day and fourteen hours of darkness. Daytime temperatures should be allowed to drop to 75°F to 85°F and nighttime temperatures can go as low as 55°F to 60°F. These conditions closely simulate the Australian spring, which is when prebreeding cycling occurs in these lizards.

Spermatogenesis in males occurs from autumn over the winter to early spring in Australia, mating occurs in the spring, and ovulation occurs shortly thereafter. Although the seasons in Australia are reversed from those in the United States, for your purposes, this is irrelevant. You are controlling conditions that simulate the seasons during which these events take place—your beardies are more concerned with the changes in condition than they are in the calendar months.

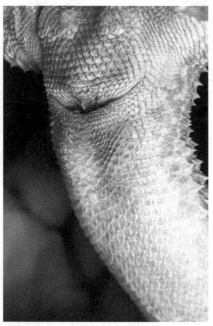

At the very top of this picture, you can see the two bulges that tell you this is a male.

In the United States, the reduced light period and temperatures may begin the first two weeks of December and be allowed to occur through mid-February. By then, you should increase the light period to fourteen hours and daytime temperatures should be returned to 85°F.

Within a month of returning to normal conditions, breeding behavior will occur. At this time, both beardies should be fed a calcium-supplemented meal once a day and a second, unsupplemented meal, if they will eat it. Females should be fed a varied, supplemented diet until the end of the summer, consisting of equal parts animal and vegetable matter at different servings.

Getting to Know You

Now you need to introduce your male and your female to each other. Think of this as a beardie blind date. Place them together in a new and very large enclosure (at

Introductions in a breeding pair must be handled carefully. Think of it as a beardie blind date.

least 5 to 6 feet long and 2 feet wide). Be sure there is a high branch for the dominant male and lower basking sites for the female. Establish separate feeding areas.

Mating will be preceded by frequent head bobbing and arm waving, as well as nipping and biting. If encounters become too aggressive and blood is drawn, it is a good idea to place the pair in separate quarters. Rearrange the setup in the breeding enclosure and reintroduce the lizards to the cage.

If you have more than one female, you may want to move two or three females in with a single male. He will mate with all the females, producing a much larger yield of offspring during this interlude, and the kind of aggressiveness seen between a single female and male placed together is less likely to occur. Even in this situation, however, fighting is not unusual and is to be expected during mating attempts.

Egg Laying

Bearded dragons are hole or burrow nesters. They will not lay their eggs until they have dug what they consider to be a suitable burrow in which to deposit them. Failure to provide the correct substrate for this purpose may stress the female and subject her to egg-binding, or dystocia (see page 109). If the substrate is too "flaky," any hole the beardie creates is apt to close up as she digs; if the substrate is too hard or compact, she will be unable to make any headway in it. A combination of sterile potting soil and sand is recommended. You should provide a heap of soil at least 8 to 12 inches deep and at least 2 to 3 feet square.

Females must dig a burrow in which to lay their eggs. Sterile potting soil mixed with sand makes a good substrate.

Although this may sound silly, you can lay out a mixture in a small area and test it yourself by digging into it with your fingers. If the hole you dig remains fairly well intact, it is suitable for bearded dragon nesting. You can leave the burrows you dug in the enclosure and introduce the female to them so she gets the idea. The time to do this is when you see her furiously rooting around for a place to dig in her normal quarters. According to commercial breeders, some females will use a man-made burrow as a starting point, dig it out the rest of the way, and deposit her eggs.

If you allow your female to dig into an outdoor enclosure with a natural substrate, be sure to flag the spot after she closes the nest so that you can remove the eggs later for artificial incubation. Leaving incubation to chance in an outdoor situation may greatly decrease the hatching success rate.

Clutch Size

The number of eggs laid by any one female bearded dragon is highly variable. Clutch size depends on a number of factors, including the female's age, physical condition, and the extent of previous breeding. Larger females between the ages of 2 and 5 years may produce thirty to fifty eggs per clutch. Smaller females may produce as many as fifty fertile eggs per season in two or three clutches.

Incubating Bearded Dragon Eggs

After your female has dug her nest and deposited her eggs, remove her from the enclosure and carefully uncover the eggs. Be careful not to rotate or turn the eggs upside down. Carefully separate and place each egg in a plastic shoebox, large plastic sweater box, or lidded plastic food dish. (Cardboard or wood containers are not recommended, as they will absorb the moisture from the substrate.) The bottom of the container should contain a 2-inch layer of vermiculite and water. This layer should be composed of equal amounts of vermiculite and water by weight: 8 ounces of vermiculite and 8 ounces of water by weight (not volume).

> **TIP**
>
> Although some breeders say Perlite may be used instead of vermiculite to incubate eggs, it was recently discovered that Perlite can emit substances noxious to eggs and can cause either death of the embryo or birth defects in hatchlings—making vermiculite a much better choice for successful breeding.

About half to two-thirds of the egg should be buried in the bed of vermiculite, with the rest of the egg left exposed on top. Place a lid on the container. The lid should have predrilled or punched-out air holes, as should the upper sides of the container. Once the eggs are placed, they should not be moved or turned.

There are now several methods you can use to incubate the eggs. You can set up a well-ventilated, temperature-controlled incubator, large enough to accommodate your boxes full of eggs; you can keep them in a place in the house where

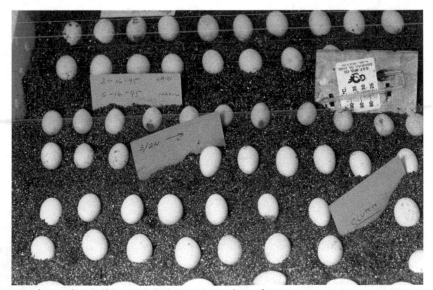

Bury the eggs about halfway in a bed of vermiculite in the incubator.

> ## Leave Outdoor Hatching to the Experts
>
> Breeders who breed beardies outdoors or in greenhouses where outdoor spring and summer temperatures are appropriate often leave their eggs in the nest and allow them to hatch naturally. Because you have little control over temperature and humidity in such a situation, there is no telling what your success rate and time to hatching will be. This is dangerous, because some hatchlings may not be able to escape either the egg or, if they get that far, they may be unable to escape the nest.

temperatures approximate those of an incubator (without the benefit of an incubator); or you can simply place the eggs in a dark, well-ventilated spot and allow them to incubate at room temperature. The warm environment of the first two options will cause the eggs to hatch more quickly than if you leave them to incubate at room temperature.

If you are going to establish an incubator with increased heat, it is important to keep that temperature between 83°F and 85°F using a thermostat. Novice breeders have learned the hard way that incubators can overheat and kill their eggs, so it is important to monitor and adjust the thermostat over a twelve-hour period *before* introducing the eggs. If your incubation period is during the warmer months, remember to keep your incubator in a room that is cooler than the incubator temperature. If the room temperature rises to 90°F or more, a thermostatically set temperature of 85°F would be easily surpassed, and you risk damaging or killing your eggs from overheating.

At higher temperatures, humidity in the vermiculite is apt to evaporate. You can help prevent this by placing a container of water in the incubator to maintain humidity levels. Check the vermiculite daily to make sure it is as damp as it was when you first set up, and refill your water container as necessary. If the vermiculite needs to be moistened, use a plant mist to moisten both the eggs and the substrate. Fertile eggs absorb water from their environment and increase in size as a result.

At about 85°F, the following incubator hatching times have been recorded (eggs incubated at cooler temperatures will take longer to hatch):

- Eastern bearded dragon (*Pogona barbata*): seventy to eighty days
- Inland bearded dragon (*Pogona vitticeps*): fifty-five to seventy-five days
- Lawson's dragon (*Pogona henrylawsoni*): forty-five to fifty-five days

Hatching Eggs

Usually, eggs hatch over twenty-four to seventy-two hours. Eggs ready to hatch will collapse or become indented. As a rule, hatching bearded dragons will slit open the egg and release themselves using a special egg tooth located just under the snout on the upper jaw. The egg tooth is lost shortly after hatching.

After most of the eggs have hatched, some collapsed but unhatched eggs may remain. The baby beardies inside may be too weak to release themselves, or may have an insufficiently developed egg tooth. You may want to assist by using a tiny pair of cuticle scissors or a small scalpel blade. Great care must be taken to cut a slit only in the egg shell and avoid injuring the infant dragon inside. The slit can be between a quarter and a third of an inch long, running along the long axis of the top of the egg.

Once you make the slit, allow the baby beardie to emerge by itself; don't attempt to pull it from the egg. A large yolk sac may remain and the lizard may not yet be ready to breathe air. Pulling it from the egg after slicing the shell can cause the baby to die. It will emerge spontaneously when it is ready.

Let the baby beardies emerge from the egg on their own.

Baby Dragons

Baby bearded dragons measure about 3 to 4 inches, including the tail, depending on the species. Body size is usually no more than 1.5 inches and birth weights range from 1.5 to 3.5 grams.

As a rule, few members of any given clutch will be born with birth defects. However, you should be aware that babies can be born with any of the following abnormalities:

- Spinal curvature or twisting
- Corkscrew spiraling of the tail
- Dom-head, where the top of the head appears enlarged or puffed out
- Leg abnormalities, including limbs that are folded in or over
- Spindly and weak limbs
- Dwarfism or failure to grow

These defects may be genetic or the result of nutritional deficits in the laying female. Incubating eggs in inadequate temperature and humidity conditions or exposing them to toxins may also result in birth defects.

Nonetheless, there is a large and growing cadre of bearded dragon breeders, resulting in the annual production of more than 100,000 of these unique and unusually calm

Bearded dragons breed well in captivity, ensuring that beardie lovers will have plenty of pets.

pet reptiles. It is fair to say that no other lizard or reptile has been so easily and successfully bred in such a short period of time as beardies. And their popularity is sure to grow over the years, as wild-caught reptiles become increasingly more difficult or illegal to obtain.

Appendix

Learning More About
Your Bearded Dragon

Some Good Books

Bartlett, Richard, and Patricia Bartlett, *Terrarium and Cage Construction and Care,* Barron's Educational Series, 1999.

De Vosjoli, Philippe, Robert Mailloux, Susan Donoghue, VMD, Roger Klingengerg, DVM, and Jerry Cole, *The Bearded Dragon Manual,* BowTie Press, 2001.

Hoser, Raymond, *Smuggled: The Underground Trade in Australia's Wildlife,* Apollo Books, 1992.

Hoser, Raymond, *Smuggled 2: Wildlife Trafficking, Crime and Corruption in Australia,* Kotaki Publishing, 1997.

Klingenberg, Roger, *Understanding Reptile Parasites: A Basic Manual for Herpetoculturists & Veterinarians,* Advanced Vivarium Systems, 1997.

Magazines

Reptiles Magazine
P.O. Box 6040
Mission Viejo, CA 92690
(800) 876-9112
www.reptilesmagazine.com

Photo Credits

Isabelle Francais: 1, 21, 22, 27, 34, 39, 42–43, 44, 46, 48, 50, 58, 60, 69, 73, 74, 76–77, 81, 85, 89, 95, 98, 109, 112, 115, 118

Howell Book House: 10

Bill Love: 4–5, 8–9,13, 14, 18, 24, 32, 45, 51, 53, 54, 67, 78, 79, 83, 92, 111, 114, 116

Tammy Rao: 11, 20, 26, 30, 31, 35, 37, 41, 56, 59, 62, 63, 65, 71, 82, 86, 87, 90, 93, 97, 100, 102, 103, 106, 108, 110, 113